rowohlt repertoire
macht Bücher wieder zugänglich,
die bislang vergriffen waren.

Freuen Sie sich auf besondere Entdeckungen
und das Wiedersehen mit Lieblingsbüchern.

Alle **rowohlt repertoire** Titel finden Sie auf
www.rowohlt.de/repertoire

Rechtschreibung und Redaktionsstand dieses Buches
entsprechen einer früher lieferbaren Ausgabe.

Veröffentlicht im Rowohlt Verlag, Reinbek bei Hamburg

Umschlaggestaltung Anzinger und Rasp, München
Druck und Bindung CPI buchbücher.de, Birkach

ISBN 978-3-688-10343-0

rowohlt repertoire

rororo sprachen
Herausgegeben von
Ludwig Moos

„Equal goes it loose“ – mit diesem vermeintlich englischen Satz soll einmal ein hochgestellter Bundesbürger bei einem Empfang der Queen seine weltläufigen Englischkenntnisse unter Beweis gestellt haben. Wer darüber ungehemmt spottet, hat die eigenen Sprachschnitzer oft nur verdrängt. Weder schlechte Zensuren noch das unter höflicher Maske erstickte Leid angelsächsischer Gesprächspartner haben verhindern können, daß sich die Deutschen immer wieder an der englischen Sprache vergehen. Nicht aus Trotz oder Dummheit, sondern weil deutsche Sprachmuster uns so prägen, machen wir stets die gleichen typischen Fehler.

Gunther Bischoff, Leiter der American School in Hamburg, hat ein Programm zum Verlernen der häufigsten Fehler entwickelt und im Unterricht erprobt. Was andere Lehrbücher vernachlässigen, wird hier zum Prinzip: Das Eingehen auf fremdsprachliche Schwierigkeiten, die aus muttersprachlichen Gewohnheiten resultieren. Bischoffs Übungsprogramm ist für Selbststudium wie Gruppenarbeit geeignet; mit seiner trial and error-Methode kann es sogar als Gesellschaftsspiel dienen. Gezielt, doch ohne ödes Pauken werden Schwächen beseitigt, die der Schüler, Tourist oder Geschäftsmann sonst auf nahezu allen Sprachniveaus beibehält.

Zum Verlernen typisch deutscher Französischfehler erscheint parallel zu diesem Band von Jacques Soussan „Pouvez-vous Français?“ (rororo sachbuch 6940). Von Gunther Bischoff gibt es einen weiteren Band, der mit der gleichen Methode den richtigen Gebrauch der schwierigen englischen Zeiten übt: „Better Times“ (rororo sachbuch 7987).

Rowohlt Verlag GmbH, Kirchenallee 19, 20099 Hamburg
Kontaktadresse nach EU-Produktsicherheitsverordnung:
produktsicherheit@rowohlt.de

TYPICAL MISTAKES

Gunther Bischoff

Speak you English?

Programmierte Übung zum Verlernen typisch deutscher Englischfehler

rororo

Rowohlt

Originalausgabe
Redaktion Ludwig Moos
Umschlagbild Gerd Huss
Umschlagentwurf Peter Wippermann

272.– 274. Tausend Mai 1997

Veröffentlicht im Rowohlt Taschenbuch Verlag GmbH,
Reinbek bei Hamburg, Mai 1974

Satz Helvetica (Linotronic 505 C)
Gesamtherstellung Clausen & Bosse, Leck
Printed in Germany
990-ISBN 3 499 16857 X

Einführung

Sie sprechen Englisch. Wahrscheinlich aber sind Sie bei dem, was Sie sagen, nie ganz sicher. Denn wie Engländer und Sprachlehrer aus leidvoller Erfahrung wissen, machen die meisten Deutschen «typische» Fehler, die anscheinend unausrottbar sind. Herkömmliche Übungsbücher und Grammatiken sind kaum geeignet, dagegen etwas zu tun. Denn sie verlangen jedem Benutzer die gleichen Lernschritte ab und nehmen keine Rücksicht darauf, ob er Japaner, Italiener oder Deutscher ist. Ein weiterer Nachteil ist, daß der Schüler meist nicht durch Üben der Sprache selbst ihre Eigenarten zu beherrschen lernt, sondern grammatikalische Abschnitte durchnimmt, deren Regeln er tunlichst auswendig zu lernen hat. Vergißt er sie, was selten ausbleibt, so liegt eine Orientierung an deutschen Sprachgewohnheiten nahe. Das aber ergibt meist kein richtiges, geschweige denn ein gutes Englisch.

Mit diesem Buch können Sie sich die häufigsten und peinlichsten Fehler, die Deutsche im Umgangsenglisch machen, abüben. Es setzt die Methode, Englisch durch Englisch zu lernen, zur «Nachbehandlung» ein, der sich alle, die Grundkenntnisse in der englischen Sprache haben, unterziehen können, die aber auch für Fortgeschrittene erfahrungsgemäß angebracht ist.

Der Aufbau des Lernprogramms beruht auf dem Prinzip von Test und Kontrolle. Beim Durcharbeiten ist zu beachten:

- Auf jeweils einer rechten Seite stehen richtige und fehlerhafte Sätze unterschiedslos nebeneinander (Übungen). Versuchen Sie rasch anzugeben, wo welcher Fehler steckt.
- Nach dem Umblättern können Sie prüfen, ob Sie richtig verbessert oder Fehler übersehen haben (Lösungen). Sie finden alle Übungssätze der vorherigen Seite wiederholt, wobei Fehlerkorrekturen halbfett hervorgehoben sind und Ziffern auf die grammatikalischen Erläuterungen im Anhang verweisen.
- Jeder fehlerhafte Satz enthält nur einen Fehler. Jeder Fehler taucht auf einer Seite nur einmal auf, wird zunächst in dichter Abfolge wiederholt und dann mit größerem Abstand – zur «Schlußkontrolle» des Übungserfolgs – noch einmal gebracht.
- Jeder Fehler wird so oft wiederholt, daß Sie ihn gründlich verlernen können. Die Wiederholungshäufigkeit stützt sich auf praktische Unterrichtserfahrungen.
- Je schneller Sie die Übungen durcharbeiten, desto wirksamer werden Sie Ihre unenglischen Sprachmuster löschen.

Elizabeth Exall, Marylla Jones und Betty Micolowsky danke ich für das englische Korrekturlesen, Regina Kobus für das Schreiben der deutschen Manuskriptteile. Sehr geholfen haben mir Iris Rabsch, die viel Zeit aufwandte, um mein verenglischtes Deutsch in deutsches Deutsch umzuwandeln, und Lucia Hammar, die in mühevoller und gründlicher Arbeit das Manuskript mit durcharbeitete.

Übung 1

1. I raised the hand, but the teacher did not see it and so did not call upon me.

2. What means the word "trouble"?

3. The tradition has been handed down from father to son since generations.

4. They don't want to have to have anything to do with him.

5. The Fifth Avenue is still the most magnificent street in the world.

6. How do you spell that word?

7. Who does not do homework will be punished.

8. He is in the enviable position of being rich.

9. In the first time I did not like the work, but then I got used to it.

10. The homework cannot be made this way.

11. Do you eat cornflakes with water and honey, or milk and sugar?

12. When the bird was alive it sang well, but when it was dead, I ate it and it tasted well.

13. I feel exhausted today because I had only three hours sleep last night.

14. While they were preparing to leave, I paced nervously up and down, smoking like a furnace.

15. Every night at 8 p.m. I hear the radio in order to learn what has happened in the world.

Lösung 1

1. I raised **my** hand, but the teacher did not see it and so did not call upon me. **1**

2. What **does** the word "trouble" **mean**? **2**

3. The tradition has been handed down from father to son **for** generations. **3**

4. They don't want to have to have anything to do with him. **4**

5. **Fifth Avenue** is still the most magnificent street in the world. **5**

6. How do you spell that word?

7. **Whoever** does not do homework will be punished. **6**

8. He is in the enviable position of being rich.

9. **At first** I did not like the work, but then I got used to it. **7**

10. The homework cannot be **done** this way. **8**

11. Do you eat cornflakes with water and honey, or milk and sugar?

12. When the bird was alive it sang well, but when it was dead, I ate it and it tasted **good**. **9**

13. I feel exhausted today because I had only three hours sleep last night.

14. While they were preparing to leave, I paced nervously up and down, smoking like a furnace.

15. Every night at 8 p.m. I **listen to** the radio in order to learn what has happened in the world. **10**

Übung 2

1. In the first time I believed his stories, but then I discovered that he was a liar.

2. At what time leaves the train the station?

3. The reporter asked the famous actor what the father had said when he first heard that his son wanted to become an actor.

4. Some of the finest shops in Hamburg are located in the Neuer Wall.

5. I don't have to have an umbrella if I have a raincoat.

6. He has been waiting at the station since two hours and no one has come to pick him up.

7. They had never been in an airplane before, so they were nervous about flying.

8. How many tickets should I buy?

9. We're going dancing after dinner. Do you want to join us?

10. Who sits at the bar must order drinks for at least five dollars.

11. If you don't keep your coat on while you are outside, you'll catch a cold.

12. Their father played football with them until dinner.

13. If you don't look out, you'll cut yourself with that big knife!

14. He always does everything right.

15. Although the movie star was not very young anymore, she dressed very well and had a beautiful figure. As a result, she still looked well.

Lösung 2

1. **At first** I believed his stories, but then I discovered that he was a liar. **7**

2. At what time **does** the train **leave** the station? **2**

3. The reporter asked the famous actor what **his** father had said when he first heard that his son wanted to become an actor. **1**

4. Some of the finest shops in Hamburg are located in **Neuer Wall.** **5**

5. I don't have to have an umbrella if I have a raincoat. **4**

6. He has been waiting at the station **for** two hours and no one has come to pick him up. **3**

7. They had never been in an airplane before, so they were nervous about flying.

8. How many tickets should I buy?

9. We're going dancing after dinner. Do you want to join us?

10. **Whoever** sits at the bar must order drinks for at least five dollars. **6**

11. If you don't keep your coat on while you are outside, you'll catch a cold.

12. Their father played football with them until dinner.

13. If you don't look out, you'll cut yourself with that big knife!

14. He always does everything right.

15. Although the movie star was not very young anymore, she dressed very well and had a beautiful figure. As a result, she still looked **good.** **9**

Übung 3

1. I see television and see a play by Shakespeare.

2. This is the most wonderful chocolate cake I have ever tasted.

3. You need a great deal of will-power to resist buying pastries in a pastry shop. The problem is that, in such a shop, it always smells so well.

4. Who does not work does not eat.

5. My son has been ill since a week, and my wife and I hope that he will not fall too far behind at school.

6. After school I often play my records and hear them.

7. If you are still sleepy at 10 a.m., you have to have a second cup of coffee.

8. One group made better work than the other.

9. It may sound very old-fashioned, but if you soak the feet in very hot water when you feel that you are catching a cold, you may find that the cold will go away.

10. How do you get to the Rathaus from here? Walk up this street until you reach the Mönckebergstrasse, turn right and continue walking straight ahead and you cannot miss it.

11. When we go on vacation our parents give us extra money.

12. Don't forget to feed the hamster while I'm gone.

13. Go you home from work at the same time every day?

14. In the first time one was shocked by the hippy's appearance, but one soon learned that he was an intelligent and likable young man.

15. Every day I am learning things I never knew before.

Lösung 3

1. I **look at** television and see a play by Shakespeare. **11**

2. This is the most wonderful chocolate cake I have ever tasted.

3. You need a great deal of will-power to resist buying pastries in a pastry shop. The problem is that, in such a shop, it always smells so **good. 9**

4. **Whoever** does not work does not eat. **6**

5. My son has been ill **for** a week, and my wife and I hope that he will not fall too far behind at school. **3**

6. After school I often play my records and **listen to** them. **10**

7. If you are still sleepy at 10 a.m., you have to have a second cup of coffee. **4**

8. One group **did** better work than the other. **8**

9. It may sound very old-fashioned, but if you soak **your** feet in very hot water when you feel that you are catching a cold, you may find that the cold will go away. **1**

10. How do you get to the Rathaus from here? Walk up this street until you reach **Mönckebergstraße,** turn right and continue walking straight ahead and you cannot miss it. **5**

11. When we go on vacation our parents give us extra money.

12. Don't forget to feed the hamster while I'm gone.

13. **Do you go** home from work at the same time every day? **2**

14. **At first** one was shocked by the hippy's appearance, but one soon learned that he was an intelligent and likable young man. **7**

15. Every day **I learn** things I never knew before. **12**

Übung 4

1. The child saw the stranger for several minutes and then began to cry.

2. Too much confusion results in many mistakes.

3. There's a wooden armchair without a seat floating down the canal.

4. How can you tell a crocodile from an alligator?

5. I have gone to India on my holidays last year, but will never go again because it is too expensive.

6. What could be made better? The planning for the future could.

7. A psychologist once humorously said that it is possible to stop a child from sucking the thumb, but it may happen that he begins to set houses on fire.

8. Since half a year the economist has been predicting bad times, but nobody has paid any attention to him.

9. The Ost-West Strasse is one of the major thoroughfares of Hamburg.

10. The steak looked well, but it was tough; therefore, the man called the waiter and requested a tender steak.

11. They have to have another room built onto their house because they are expecting another child.

12. I won't hear you any more. You say nothing but nonsense.

13. In the first time there was very little to do at the office, but then the orders began pouring in and all the employees had to work overtime.

14. Every weekday morning I am leaving for work at exactly 7:15 a.m.

15. Who says such a thing does not know what he is talking about.

Lösung 4

1. The child **looked at** the stranger for several minutes and then began to cry. **11**

2. Too much confusion results in many mistakes.

3. There's a wooden armchair without a seat floating down the canal.

4. How can you tell a crocodile from an alligator?

5. I **went** to India on my holidays last year, but will never go again because it is too expensive. **13**

6. What could be **done** better? The planning for the future could. **8**

7. A psychologist once humorously said that it is possible to stop a child from sucking **his** thumb, but it may happen that he begins to set houses on fire. **1**

8. **For** half a year the economist has been predicting bad times, but nobody has paid any attention to him. **3**

9. **Ost-West Strasse** is one of the major thoroughfares of Hamburg. **5**

10. The steak looked **good,** but is was tough; therefore, the man called the waiter and requested a tender steak.. **9**

11. They have to have another room built onto their house because they are expecting another child. **4**

12. I won't **listen to** you any more. You say nothing but nonsense. **10**

13. **At first** there was very little to do at the office, but then the orders began pouring in and all the employees had to work overtime. **7**

14. Every weekday morning I **leave** for work at exactly 7:15 a.m. **12**

15. **Whoever** says such a thing does not know what he is talking about. **6**

Übung 5

1. John has not been here last week so I have not been able to give him your regards.

2. Her dearest possession was a miniature orange tree, which she watered faithfully every day.

3. An angry bull broke out of the pasture and charged a car as it was driving down the quiet country lane.

4. There was not some salt on the table so I called the waiter.

5. See outside to see if it is raining. If it is, I must wear boots.

6. It was his meaning that things had to be changed.

7. She's a nice neighbour. She really hears you when you tell her your problems.

8. The answer was on the tip of my tongue, but when the teacher actually called on me, I forgot what I was going to say.

9. I was happy while I was learning English in the Deich Strasse.

10. To do a thing correctly you have to have enough time.

11. What costs a glass of beer at the Four Seasons Hotel?

12. In the first time I thought that it would be impossible to get the work completed on time, but then I realized that we would be finished on schedule.

13. Surely what you are telling me now isn't true! You're only pulling my leg!

14. If a housewife makes all her cleaning in the morning, then she has the whole afternoon for her private interests.

15. It feels well to take a hot shower after a hard day's work.

Lösung 5

1. John **was not** here last week so I have not been able to give him your regards. **13**

2. Her dearest possession was a miniature orange tree, which she watered faithfully every day.

3. An angry bull broke out of the pasture and charged a car as it was driving down the quiet country lane.

4. There was not **any** salt on the table so I called the waiter. **14**

5. **Look** outside to see if it is raining. If it is, I must wear boots. **11**

6. It was his **opinion** that things had to be changed. **15**

7. She's a nice neighbour. She really **listens to** you when you tell her your problems. **10**

8. The answer was on the tip of my tongue, but when the teacher actually called on me, I forgot what I was going to say.

9. I was happy while I was learning English in **Deich Strasse.** **5**

10. To do a thing correctly you have to have enough time. **4**

11. What **does** a glass of beer **cost** at the Four Seasons Hotel? **2**

12. **At first** I thought that it would be impossible to get the work completed on time, but then I realized that we would be finished on schedule. **7**

13. Surely what you are telling me now isn't true! You're only pulling my leg!

14. If a housewife **does** all her cleaning in the morning, then she has the whole afternoon for her private interests. **8**

15. It feels **good** to take a hot shower after a hard day's work. **9**

Übung 6

1. Who works an eight hour day will never become a manager.

2. I don't think something can be done to solve the problem.

3. It was his meaning all along that the company's policies were wrong.

4. The man looked very silly because the barber had cut the hair too short.

5. A real athlete is not smoking cigarettes.

6. The diver has been under water since twenty minutes and has found nothing.

7. Cats like to be appreciated quietly, but dogs like demonstrative affection.

8. Don't see into my room! I'm wrapping Christmas presents, and I don't want you to know what I'm going to give you.

9. Are you hearing, Johnny? I said GO TO BED!

10. The manager has made so many mistakes last year that it is not reasonable to expect his successor to put the situation in order overnight.

11. Siamese cats have crossed eyes.

12. You don't have to have everything other people have to be happy.

13. Of course pupils learn a great deal at school, but if they don't make homework they don't learn so much at school as they could.

14. The only way to get to my house is to walk down the Lexington Avenue until you can go no farther. It is the last house on the right.

15. In the first time the young man hesitated to ask the beautiful girl to go out with him, but then he overcame his shyness and got a date.

Lösung 6

1. **Whoever** works an eight hour day will never become a manager. **6**

2. I don't think **anything** can be done to solve the problem. **14**

3. It was his **opinion** all along that the company's policies were wrong. **15**

4. The man looked very silly because the barber had cut **his** hair too short. **1**

5. A real athlete **does not smoke** cigarettes. **12**

6. The diver has been under water **for** twenty minutes and has found nothing. **3**

7. Cats like to be appreciated quietly, but dogs like demonstrative affection.

8. Don't **look** into my room! I'm wrapping Christmas presents, and I don't want you to know what I'm going to give you. **11**

9. Are you **listening,** Johnny? I said GO TO BED! **10**

10. The manager **made** so many mistakes last year that it is not reasonable to expect his successor to put the situation in order overnight. **13**

11. Siamese cats have crossed eyes.

12. You don't have to have everything other people have to be happy. **4**

13. Of course pupils learn a great deal at school, but if they don't **do** homework they don't learn so much at school as they could. **8**

14. The only way to get to my house is to walk down **Lexington Avenue** until you can go no farther. It is the last house on the right. **5**

15. **At first** the young man hesitated to ask the beautiful girl to go out with him, but then he overcame his shyness and got a date. **7**

Übung 7

1. We drove past a car with a dog seeing out of the rear window.

2. Why is it that I am seldom getting sleepy when it is time to go to bed?

3. Has not the politician said just yesterday, that the project would cost the taxpayer too much? If so, why is he recommending the same project today?

4. I put my hands into the pockets and walked away.

5. In the first time I thought that the job was the same as the ones I had handled before; then I saw that it was not only more difficult, but more dangerous as well.

6. Understood I correctly when I heard you say you had just won half a million in the lottery?

7. They spent the afternoon walking happily along the river – until they fell in.

8. They were very lucky because they could find anyone to replace him.

9. Most big firms have a special research and development department which makes the planning for the products of the future.

10. It takes a long time to train a dog to obey you. You need to have a lot of patience.

11. Who drives his car too quickly must expect to pay a fine.

12. My meaning is that you never get anything for nothing.

13. Hear carefully while I explain what you must do.

14. To dress expensively is not necessarily the same as to dress good.

15. The new motor had only been running since five hours when it stopped.

Lösung 7

1. We drove past a car with a dog **looking** out of the rear window. **11**

2. Why is it that I **seldom get** sleepy when it is time to go to bed? **12**

3. **Did** not the politician **say** just yesterday that the project would cost the taxpayer too much? If so, why is he recommending the same project today? **13**

4. I put my hands into **my** pockets and walked away. **1**

5. **At first** I thought that the job was the same as the ones I had handled before; then I saw that it was not only more difficult, but more dangerous as well. **7**

6. **Did I understand** correctly when I heard you say you had just won half a million in the lottery? **2**

7. They spent the afternoon walking happily along the river – until they fell in.

8. They were very lucky because they could find **someone** to replace him. **14**

9. Most big firms have a special research and development department which **does** the planning for the products of the future. **8**

10. It takes a long time to train a dog to obey you. You need to have a lot of patience.

11. **Whoever** drives his car too quickly must expect to pay a fine. **6**

12. My **opinion** is that you never get anything for nothing. **15**

13. **Listen** carefully while I explain what you must do. **10**

14. To dress expensively is not necessarily the same as to dress **well.** **9**

15. The new motor had only been running **for** five hours when it stopped. **3**

Übung 8

1. Is there something you can do to help someone who does not want your help?

2. How much beer can you drink before you become unsteady on your feet?

3. An owl has excellent night vision. A cat sees good at night, too.

4. I must say that the pupil has learned a lot at the refresher course he attended last month.

5. Don't touch this machine. It is very sensitive and may explode if not handled carefully!

6. The children saw into the refrigerator to find ice cream, but there wasn't any left.

7. He refused our offer even though it was a good one.

8. His meaning was that he was right even though everyone else thought that he was wrong.

9. Only princesses in fairy tales marry frogs who change into princes.

10. The wedding card that they had tried to send her was returned by the post office because they'd forgotten the stamp.

11. The statistics show that the sun shone since twenty-three consecutive days in Hamburg last April.

12. If you don't hurry up, the train will leave without us.

13. Immediately before my holidays I am never leaving my office before 8 p.m. because I must make arrangements for the time I will be gone.

14. It's not good for your body when you eat a lot of salt.

15. How much costs an apartment in Hamburg?

Lösung 8

1. Is there **anything** you can do to help someone who does not want your help? **14**

2. How much beer can you drink before you become unsteady on your feet?

3. An owl has excellent night vision. A cat sees **well** at night, too. **9**

4. I must say that the pupil **learned** a lot at the refresher course he attended last month. **13**

5. Don't touch this machine. It is very sensitive and may explode if not handled carefully!

6. The children **looked** into the refrigerator to find ice cream, but there wasn't any left. **11**

7. He refused our offer even though it was a good one.

8. His **opinion** was that he was right even though everyone else thought that he was wrong. **15**

9. Only princesses in fairy tales marry frogs who change into princes.

10. The wedding card that they had tried to send her was returned by the post office because they'd forgotten the stamp.

11. The statistics show that the sun shone **for** twenty-three consecutive days in Hamburg last April. **3**

12. If you don't hurry up, the train will leave without us.

13. Immediately before my holidays I **never leave** my office before 8 p.m. because I must make arrangements for the time I will be gone. **12**

14. It's not good for your body when you eat a lot of salt.

15. How much **does** an apartment in Hamburg **cost?** **2**

Übung 9

1. I cannot speak French and you also cannot speak French.

2. The old lady was in such a hurry that she slipped and fell, dropping her groceries and tearing her stocking.

3. I've never seen a purple cow. Have you?

4. While leaning out of the window, we saw a strange-looking man picking roses and putting them into a bag.

5. The man that you met on the street yesterday is my brother.

6. I don't want a picture of your grandmother! It is not worth something to me because I don't know her.

7. For two years I started learning English.

8. It is equal whether the work is done by a man or a woman, as long as it is done well.

9. I have driven always my car to work and have never had an accident.

10. We didn't expect so much people at the party.

11. The spider climbed slowly up the wall until it reached the corner where it had made its web.

12. Until we replace the broken light bulb, we won't be able to read in this room.

13. Hurry up and come downstairs, or it will be too late to help me.

14. My meaning is that she's not good enough for him.

15. It is time for you and I to go home now, for it is late.

Lösung 9

1. I cannot speak French and you cannot speak French **either.** **16**

2. The old lady was in such a hurry that she slipped and fell, dropping her groceries and tearing her stocking.

3. I've never seen a purple cow. Have you?

4. While leaning out of the window, we saw a strange-looking man picking roses and putting them into a bag.

5. The man that you met on the street yesterday is my brother. **17**

6. I don't want a picture of your grandmother! It is not worth **anything** to me because I don't know her. **14**

7. **Two years ago** I started learning English. **18**

8. It **doesn't matter** whether the work is done by a man or a woman, as long as it is done well. **19**

9. I have **always driven** my car to work and have never had an accident. **20**

10. We didn't expect so **many** people at the party. **21**

11. The spider climbed slowly up the wall until it reached the corner where it had made its web.

12. Until we replace the broken light bulb, we won't be able to read in this room.

13. Hurry up and come downstairs, or it will be too late to help me.

14. My **opinion** is that she's not good enough for him. **15**

15. It is time for you and **me** to go home now, for it is late. **22**

Übung 10

1. The woman that was hit by the car is now in the hospital.

2. You are not going to the cinema and I am not going to the cinema, too.

3. The secretary was moved often from office to office.

4. Are you always taking your holidays in the mountains?

5. That joke is old. I heard it for the first time for five years.

6. It was the thief's meaning that the shop could only be robbed at night. Otherwise, the robbers would be seen and caught.

7. In 1950, 5,000 less people were struck by this illness than a decade before.

8. The only way the explorers could survive the extreme cold of the South Pole was to dress in many layers of fur.

9. It is difficult not to be surprised by the appearance of a ghost even if you are in a haunted house and expect to see one.

10. A picture fell down from the bedroom wall during the night, and scared her to death.

11. You may disagree, but I don't think there is something interesting about learning English.

12. Riding a bicycle in the rain is unpleasant.

13. It's not easy to stand on your head and smoke at the same time. The ashes fall into your hair.

14. When you feel angry, it helps to say so.

15. I have not seen the changing of the guard while I was in London last summer because I spent too much time at the Tower of London.

Lösung 10

1. The woman that was hit by the car is now in the hospital. **17**

2. You are not going to the cinema and I am not going to the cinema, **either.** **16**

3. The secretary was **often moved** from office to office. **20**

4. **Do you always take** your holidays in the mountains? **12**

5. That joke is old. I heard it for the first time **five years ago.** **18**

6. It was the thief's **opinion** that the shop could only be robbed at night. Otherwise, the robbers would be seen and caught. **15**

7. In 1950, 5,000 **fewer** people were struck by this illness than a decade before. **21**

8. The only way the explorers could survive the extreme cold of the South Pole was to dress in many layers of fur.

9. It is difficult not to be surprised by the appearance of a ghost even if you are in a haunted house and expect to see one.

10. A picture fell down from the bedroom wall during the night, and scared her to death.

11. You may disagree, but I don't think there is **anything** interesting about learning English. **14**

12. Riding a bicycle in the rain is unpleasant.

13. It's not easy to stand on your head and smoke at the same time. The ashes fall into your hair.

14. When you feel angry, it helps to say so.

15. I **didn't see** the changing of the guard while I was in London last summer because I spent too much time at the Tower of London. **13**

Übung 11

1. If you think back you will remember that he told you and I that it was not necessary to be at his home at exactly 8 p.m., although the party would officially begin at that time.

2. The first thing I do when I get up in the morning is to wash me.

3. In general it is equal to me whether I spend my holidays at the seaside or in the mountains. What is important is that I get my rest.

4. I came to Hamburg for 15 years.

5. I am right always when I guess how old a person is.

6. She is married to a baron and lives in a castle in Scotland.

7. Our problem is that we do too less grammar.

8. New York is a city of nine millions.

9. If you have no money, what happens to me quite often, you will just have to work for a change.

10. His father didn't go to college and his mother didn't go, too.

11. The man that had escaped from jail was caught five hours later.

12. Come and sit beside me near the fire. There is room here for another person besides me!

13. Why is it always necessary to tell the truth? Tactfulness is worth anything, too. Yet tactfulness is also a kind of lying, isn't it?

14. The simplicity of the Japanese room pleased us.

15. On the weekends, I am usually working in the garden, especially when the weather is good.

Lösung 11

1. If you think back you will remember that he told you and **me** that it was not necessary to be at his home at exactly 8 p.m., although the party would officially begin at that time. **22**

2. The first thing I do when get up in the morning is to wash **myself.** **23**

3. In general it **doesn't matter** whether I spend my holidays at the seaside or in the mountains. What is importaht is that I get my rest. **19**

4. I came to Hamburg **15 years ago.** **18**

5. I am **always right** when I guess how old a person is. **20**

6. She is married to a baron and lives in a castle in Scotland.

7. Our problem is that we do too **little** grammar. **21**

8. New York is a city of nine **million.** **24**

9. If you have no money, **which** happens to me quite often, you will just have to work for a change. **25**

10. His father didn't go to college and his mother didn't go, **either.** **16**

11. The man that had escaped from jail was caught five hours later. **17**

12. Come and sit beside me near the fire. There is room here for another person besides me!

13. Why is it always necessary to tell the truth? Tactfulness is worth **something**, too. Yet tactfulness is also a kind of lying, isn't it? **14**

14. The simplicity of the Japanese room pleased us.

15. On the weekends, I **usually work** in the garden, especially when the weather is good. **12**

Übung 12

1. We will inform us about the problem and see if there is anything we can do to remedy the situation.

2. If you find it hard to go to work, what is mostly the case on Mondays, remember that it is the same for most people.

3. I believe that it is dangerous to stick your head out of train windows. What if another train passes very close to your train?

4. Whatever troubles you at night will always seem better in the morning.

5. Good friends are hard to find, and sometimes hard to keep.

6. The Second World War ended for many years and it is high time to forget old disputes and rivalries.

7. He is a 19-years-old boy.

8. For people who love their work, it is equal whether the weather is good or bad.

9. The woman was called fat by another woman that, ironically, was even fatter than she was.

10. He exploded with a sneeze that shook the whole room.

11. The fact of the matter is that nobody informed my wife and I that the meeting was being postponed till the following week.

12. I don't like to clean other people's houses.

13. First we noticed that the table was not well made and then that the chairs were not well made, too.

14. I am early never.

15. If you have a job which pays well, you have no time to go on long trips.

Lösung 12

1. We will inform **ourselves** about the problem and see if there is anything we can do to remedy the situation. **23**

2. If you find it hard to go to work, **which** is mostly the case on Mondays, remember that it is the same for most people. **25**

3. I believe that it is dangerous to stick your head out of train windows. What if another train passes very close to your train?

4. Whatever troubles you at night will always seem better in the morning.

5. Good friends are hard to find, and sometimes hard to keep.

6. The Second World War ended **many years ago** and it is high time to forget old disputes and rivalries. **18**

7. He is a **19-year-old** boy. **24**

8. For people who love their work, it **doesn't matter** whether the weather is good or bad. **19**

9. The woman was called fat by another woman that, ironically, was even fatter than she was. **17**

10. He exploded with a sneeze that shook the whole room.

11. The fact of the matter is that nobody informed my wife and **me** that the meeting was being postponed till the following week. **22**

12. I don't like to clean other people's houses.

13. First we noticed that the table was not well made and then that the chairs were not well made, **either.** **16**

14. I am **never early.** **20**

15. If you have a job which pays well, you have no time to go on long trips.

Übung 13

1. The fisherman ate seldom fish.

2. Not to make a mental note of a person's name, what I mostly fail to do, often results in an embarrassing situation.

3. Children think that it is equal whether or not they wash their hands before they eat.

4. The last time the famous author was seen in public was in a bistro for seven years.

5. If there are 20 chairs in the large room and 5 chairs in the small room, then there are more chairs in the large room than in the small one, and less chairs in the small room than in the large one.

6. Don't eat that fruit until you have washed it.

7. After the king had had his prime minister beheaded for treason, he didn't like him very much.

8. A ten-years-old dog is comparable in age to a fifty-years-old man.

9. If we don't find a good excuse, Harry, you can be sure that the blame will be put on you and I as usual.

10. She didn't have anything to wear to the party, so she didn't go.

11. She doesn't like the color pink, and I don't, too.

12. He often argued with his tax consultant.

13. She learned through a private detective that her husband was having an affair with a woman that was ten years younger than she was.

14. A good sense of humour always helps a person cope with life.

15. People who are always in a hurry sometimes miss seeing things they would enjoy looking at.

Lösung 13

1. The fisherman **seldom ate** fish. **20**

2. Not to make a mental note of a person's name, **which** I mostly fail to do, often results in an embarrassing situation. **25**

3. Children think that it **doesn't matter** whether or not they wash their hands before they eat. **19**

4. The last time the famous author was seen in public was in a bistro **seven years ago. 18**

5. If there are 20 chairs in the large room and 5 chairs in the small room, then there are more chairs in the large room than in the small one, and **fewer** chairs in the small room than in the large one. **21**

6. Don't eat that fruit until you have washed it.

7. After the king had had his prime minister beheaded for treason, he didn't like **himself** very much. **23**

8. A **ten-year-old** dog is comparable in age to a **fifty-year-old** man. **24**

9. If we don't find a good excuse, Harry, you can be sure that the blame will be put on you and **me** as usual. **22**

10. She didn't have anything to wear to the party, so she didn't go.

11. She doesn't like the color pink, and I don't, **either. 16**

12. He often argued with his tax consultant.

13. She learned through a private detective that her husband was having an affair with a woman that was ten years younger than she was. **17**

14. A good sense of humour always helps a person cope with life.

15. People who are always in a hurry sometimes miss seeing things they would enjoy looking at.

Übung 14

1. I can't stand coffee without milk and sugar.

2. Someone ought to invent a pair of windshield-wipers for glasses.

3. He would have been always happy if he had been rich.

4. If you think that it is equal whether you make grammatical mistakes or not, I can assure you that you are wrong.

5. If too much people have too little bread, it is only a matter of time before you have a revolution on your hands.

6. He never eats dinner on weekdays, and we don't, also.

7. You can't do this to Betty and I. If you try, we will get a lawyer and sue you.

8. That telephone call just reminded me of a call I must make.

9. A new era began for international trade with the introduction of container shipping for eight years.

10. The protesters write disapproving letters in always increasing numbers.

11. To attempt to lose weight by exercising on the weekend, what many middle-aged men attempt to do, is a hopeless effort if not supported by dieting during the week.

12. Among the students there are only five that are from abroad.

13. If we inform us about hotel vacancies two months in advance, we should not have any trouble getting reservations.

14. The sun shined all day yesterday.

15. Climbing the tree, the kitten suddenly got frightened, and began to mew for help.

Lösung 14

1. I can't stand coffee without milk and sugar.

2. Someone ought to invent a pair of windshield-wipers for glasses.

3. He would **always have been** happy if he had been rich. **20**

4. If you think that it **doesn't matter** whether you make grammatical mistakes or not, I can assure you that you are wrong. **19**

5. If too **many** people have too little bread, it is only a matter of time before you have a revolution on your hands. **21**

6. He never eats dinner on weekdays, and we don't, **either.** **16**

7. You can't do this to Betty and **me.** If you try, we will get a lawyer and sue you. **22**

8. That telephone call just reminded me of a call I must make.

9. A new era began for international trade with the introduction of container shipping **eight years ago.** **18**

10. The protesters write disapproving letters in **ever** increasing numbers. **26**

11. To attempt to lose weight by exercising on the weekend, **which** many middle-aged men attempt to do, is a hopeless effort if not supported by dieting during the week. **25**

12. Among the students there are only five that are from abroad. **17**

13. If we inform **ourselves** about hotel vacancies two months in advance, we should not have any trouble getting reservations. **23**

14. The sun **shone** all day yesterday. **27**

15. Climbing the tree, the kitten suddenly got frightened, and began to mew for help.

Übung 15

1. Stuttgart's main attraction 15 years ago was a two hundred-meters-high television tower.

2. He will go to visit his mother even though he doesn't want to.

3. The police discovered with horror that the car involved in the accident had been driven by a man that was almost blind.

4. Thank you for having helped my brother and I in this matter.

5. She wants him to kiss her.

6. I will need a lot of luck, so please cross the fingers for me.

7. For Christmas my grandmother knitted sweaters for my sister and me.

8. To tell a lie when in an awkward situation, what is done by people who lack self-confidence, can only lead to a loss of trust.

9. If that tea stays in the teapot any longer, it'll be so strong you won't be able to drink it.

10. If there are too little complaints, the owner of a business may not know what the customer does not like, and lose him. Complaints are necessary if a business is to be successful.

11. For some people it is equal whether they hurt others or not, just as long as they get what they want.

12. I want to arrange things for me.

13. A car is not only useful for business purposes; you can use it also for excursions on the weekend.

14. Please get the newspaper for me from the porch where the paperboy left it.

15. I work better when there is music in the background.

Lösung 15

1. Stuttgart's main attraction 15 years ago was a **two hundred-meter-high** television tower. **24**

2. He will go to visit his mother even though he doesn't want to.

3. The police discovered with horror that the car involved in the accident had been driven by a man that was almost blind. **17**

4. Thank you for having helped my brother and **me** in this matter. **22**

5. She wants him to kiss her.

6. I will need a lot of luck, so please cross **your** fingers for me. **1**

7. For Christmas my grandmother knitted sweaters for my sister and me.

8. To tell a lie when in an awkward situation, **which** is done by people who lack self-confidence, can only lead to a loss of trust. **25**

9. If that tea stays in the teapot any longer, it'll be so strong you won't be able to drink it.

10. If there are too **few** complaints, the owner of a business may not know what the customer does not like, and lose him. Complaints are necessary if a business is to be successful. **21**

11. For some people it **doesn't matter** whether they hurt others or not, just as long as they get what they want. **19**

12. I want to arrange things for **myself.** **23**

13. A car is not only useful for business purposes; you can **also use it** for excursions on the weekend. **20**

14. Please get the newspaper for me from the porch where the paperboy left it.

15. I work better when there is music in the background.

Übung 16

1. The way to a long and happy life is to eat no meat.

2. The child always said his prayers before he went to bed.

3. Her ring was too small for her, so she had to use soap to get it off her finger.

4. I don't care what you say. Fifty coats are too much coats to hang in such a little room.

5. The newly polished floor shined.

6. How do you call a thing that has four legs and a top? It is called a "table."

7. We ever hope for peace.

8. The unions are trying to get industry to accept a thirty-five-hours week.

9. Their teacher always gives credit where credit is due.

10. Mothers often blame the elder child for starting a fight when it is the younger child who began the fight.

11. A good singer breathes deeply, and has good posture.

12. To fall in love with one person after the other, what often happens among teenagers, should not be taken too seriously.

13. The Grosse Freiheit has a big reputation for such a small street.

14. We are sorry to say that we do not have the desired information, but we will inform us and send you the facts as soon as possible.

15. Only people with pleasant voices and good reading ability should try to read the news at a radio station.

Lösung 16

1. The way to a long and happy life is to eat no meat.

2. The child always said his prayers before he went to bed.

3. Her ring was too small for her, so she had to use soap to get it off her finger.

4. I don't care what you say. Fifty coats are too **many coats** to hang in such a little room. **21**

5. The newly polished floor **shone.** **27**

6. **What** do you call a thing that has four legs and a top? It is called a "table." **28**

7. We **always** hope for peace. **26**

8. The unions are trying to get industry to accept a **thirty-five-hour** week. **24**

9. Their teacher always gives credit where credit is due.

10. Mothers often blame the elder child for starting a fight when it is the younger child who began the fight.

11. A good singer breathes deeply, and has good posture.

12. To fall in love with one person after the other, **which** often happens among teenagers, should not be taken too seriously. **25**

13. **Grosse Freiheit** has a big reputation for such a small street. **5**

14. We are sorry to say that we do not have the desired information, but we will inform **ourselves** and send you the facts as soon as possible. **23**

15. Only people with pleasant voices and good reading ability should try to read the news at a radio station.

Übung 17

1. He got down on his knees and begged me to help him, but I didn't like to get involved in such a situation, so I refused.

2. Look, here is a book of me that I thought I had lost.

3. He spoke well but I did not understand him because he used words I never heard before.

4. You may as well forget about trying to get that grouchy man to participate in our picnic plans.

5. He certainly hit the nail on the head when he called her a born athlete. She has had good coordination since she was a baby, and has always been strong and active.

6. How do we call a thing that has no name?

7. Although it is not very long, a three-weeks holiday does make a difference.

8. They raised goats for milk, and sold it to their neighbours, too.

9. No Hamburg taxi driver will bring you to Quickborn for less than DM 20,–.

10. Since the party began at 8:00 p.m., and M. Jones arrived at 8:15 p.m., he was 15 minutes too late.

11. He had talked about moving for ten years before he finally did it.

12. Whistle if you must, but please try to stay in tune.

13. The young woman would have been quite pretty if she had had a pleasant expression.

14. The advantage of the manager is that he can overlook the whole.

15. The new light bulb shined brightly.

Lösung 17

1. He got down on his knees and begged me to help him, but I didn't **want** to get involved in such a situation, so I refused. **29**

2. Look, here is a book of **mine** that I thought I had lost. **30**

3. He spoke well, but I did not understand him because he used words I **had never heard** before. **31**

4. You may as well forget about trying to get that grouchy man to participate in our picnic plans.

5. He certainly hit the nail on the head when he called her a born athlete. She has had good coordination since she was a baby, and has always been strong and active.

6. **What** do we call a thing that has no name? **28**

7. Although it is not very long, a **three-week** holiday does make a difference. **24**

8. They raised goats for milk, and sold it to their neighbours, too.

9. No Hamburg taxi driver will **take** you to Quickborn for less than DM 20,–. **32**

10. Since the party began at 8:00 p.m., and M. Jones arrived at 8:15 p.m., he was 15 minutes **late.** **33**

11. He had talked about moving for ten years before he finally did it.

12. Whistle if you must, but please try to stay in tune.

13. The young woman would have been quite pretty if she had had a pleasant expression.

14. The advantage of the manager is that he can **oversee** the whole. **35**

15. The new light bulb **shone** brightly. **27**

Übung 18

1. I simply didn't like to lend him the money, so I refused.
2. How do you call it when one football player throws the football to another player? It's called a "pass."
3. I ever think of you when I see spring flowers.
4. I'd rather clean a bird cage than a horse's stable, but I like horses better than birds.
5. Her desire for fine clothes and expensive furniture drove her into debt.
6. The child's face shined with happiness.
7. I told her that I would bring her home after the party.
8. When he was small, he pretended he was an airplane pilot.
9. With perspiration dripping from his face, he came tearing up the stairs, two steps at a time.
10. People who burn trash make the air smell awful.
11. The workers only returned to work after a crippling fifty-days strike that cost an estimated seventy-five million dollars in lost production.
12. Do birds sing beautifully because they eat flowers?
13. The cowboy whipped out his pistol and shot at the bad guy, but he missed.
14. If you don't have the keys, it's not my fault! I have already given them to you.
15. Because the man had got into a traffic jam that morning, he arrived at his office a bit too late.

Lösung 18

1. I simply didn't **want** to lend him the money, so I refused. **29**

2. **What** do you call it when one football player throws the football to another player? It's called a "pass." **28**

3. I **always** think of you when I see spring flowers. **26**

4. I'd rather clean a bird cage than a horse's stable, but I like horses better than birds.

5. Her desire for fine clothes and expensive furniture drove her into debt.

6. The child's face **shone** with happiness. **27**

7. I told her that I would **take** her home after the party. **32**

8. When he was small, he pretended he was an airplane pilot.

9. With perspiration dripping from has face, he came tearing up the stairs, two steps at a time.

10. People who burn trash make the air smell awful.

11. The workers only returned to work after a crippling **fifty-day** strike that cost an estimated seventy-five million dollars in lost production. **24**

12. Do birds sing beautifully because they eat flowers?

13. The cowboy whipped out his pistol and shot at the bad guy, but he missed.

14. If you don't have the keys, it's not my fault! I have already given them to you.

15. Because the man had got into a traffic jam that morning, he arrived at his office a bit **late.** **33**

Übung 19

1. The group of sailors I passed on the street was speaking Spanish.

2. I am really discouraged because I ever seem to find new problems just when my troubles seem to be over.

3. The full moon shined into my window.

4. What you have said is only another lousy trick of you. I don't believe you.

5. The teacher came to class half an hour too late.

6. The parents didn't like their daughter to get married because they felt that twenty was too young.

7. I'll attend your wedding, come what may.

8. Because the child was in a hurry, he left the water running in the sink and it overflowed and covered the kitchen floor.

9. How do you call the holiday that falls on December 25th? It is Christmas, of course.

10. To get what he wanted, he thought he had to use violence.

11. To overlook a situation one must consider all points of view.

12. When you lose a tooth, put it under your pillow and you'll find it exchanged for a piece of gold during the night by a fairy.

13. Most people don't know what they want.

14. The traffic in most big cities is getting worse and worse.

15. A mirror image is rather like a shadow, and also a bit like an echo.

Lösung 19

1. The group of sailors I passed on the street was speaking Spanish.

2. I am really discouraged because I **always** seem to find new problems just when my troubles seem to be over. **26**

3. The full moon **shone** into my window. **27**

4. What you have said is only another lousy trick of **yours.** I don't believe you. **30**

5. The teacher came to class half an hour **late.** **33**

6. The parents didn't **want** their daughter to get married because they felt that twenty was too young. **29**

7. I'll attend your wedding, come what may.

8. Because the child was in a hurry, he left the water running in the sink and it overflowed and covered the kitchen floor.

9. **What** do you call the holiday that falls on December 25th? It is Christmas, of course. **28**

10. To get what he wanted, he thought he had to use violence.

11. To **oversee** a situation one must consider all points of view. **35**

12. When you lose a tooth, put it under your pillow and you'll find it exchanged for a piece of gold during the night by a fairy.

13. Most people don't know what they want.

14. The traffic in most big cities is getting worse and worse.

15. A mirror image is rather like a shadow, and also a bit like an echo.

Übung 20

1. He ever asks stupid questions.

2. If you bring the bottles back to the shop, you will get a refund.

3. How do we call it when a parent beats his child too often and too hard? We call it "child abuse."

4. Before I came to Germany I never spoke German.

5. Between the two huge ocean liners, one from China and one from Spain, came a tiny sailboat.

6. After repairing the copy machine, his hands were covered with grease.

7. It is extremely difficult to think of sentences when one has no particular problem with which to deal.

8. I didn't believe him because what he said sounded suspicious to me. Besides, he had a dishonest look about him.

9. The woman did not show much enthusiasm when her neighbour told her the gossip, because she didn't like to get involved with her neighbour's problems.

10. Her new bright red shoes shined.

11. She burned the rice.

12. While I walked in the park yesterday I saw a St. Bernard dog that was as large as a pony.

13. The wolves howled at the full moon.

14. The usher told me that if I would come to the theatre early, I would get a better seat.

15. I think it was a decision of him to hold the meeting at a restaurant instead of at the firm.

Lösung 20

1. He **always** asks stupid questions. **26**

2. If you **take** the bottles back to the shop, you will get a refund. **32**

3. **What** do we call it when a parent beats his child too often and too hard? We call it "child abuse." **28**

4. Before I came to Germany I **had never spoken** German. **31**

5. Between the two huge ocean liners, one from China and one from Spain, came a tiny sailboat.

6. After repairing the copy machine, his hands were covered with grease.

7. It is extremely difficult to think of sentences when one has no particular problem with which to deal.

8. I didn't believe him because what he said sounded suspicious to me. Besides, he had a dishonest look about him.

9. The woman did not show much enthusiasm when her neighbour told her the gossip, because she didn't **want** to get involved with her neighbour's problems. **29**

10. Her new bright red shoes **shone.** **27**

11. She burned the rice.

12. While I **was walking** in the park yesterday I saw a St. Bernard dog that was as large as a pony. **36**

13. The wolves howled at the full moon.

14. The usher told me that if I **came** to the theatre early, I would get a better seat. **37**

15. I think it was a decision of **his** to hold the meeting at a restaurant instead of at the firm. **30**

Übung 21

1. While I waited for my bus to come, it began to rain.

2. I am used to live alone and so I don't get lonely.

3. Unless we hurry we'll be too late to the meeting.

4. Mary Poppins slid down the banister carrying her umbrella with its parrot handle and her briefcase.

5. My sister and I were full of ideas when we were young. She thought we should abolish cars and make everyone ride bicycles to work. Now she has a car herself, and has forgotten that old idea of her.

6. If you train your English every day, instead of once a week, you will learn much more quickly.

7. She practices the piano every afternoon, come hell or high water.

8. How do we call the two children's diseases that cover the victim with red spots? We call them measles and chickenpox.

9. The general had to overlook the movements of three divisions.

10. If I would not have seen the car coming and been able to jump aside, I would have been killed.

11. He who doesn't have a chance to express himself is always frustrated.

12. They did not like him to make a mistake.

13. He likes eating sugar cubes because he likes the way they crunch.

14. An early American pioneer woke up one morning with part of his beard gone because a curious mouse had nibbled some of it during the night.

15. It was terribly embarrassing to discover that I had no money in my pocket to pay the bill at the restaurant. Such a thing never happened to me before.

Lösung 21

1. While I **was waiting** for my bus to come, it began to rain. **36**

2. I am used to **living** alone and so I don't get lonely. **38**

3. Unless we hurry we'll be **late** to the meeting. **33**

4. Mary Poppins slid down the banister carrying her umbrella with its parrot handle and her briefcase.

5. My sister and I were full of ideas when we were young. She thought we should abolish cars and make everyone ride bicycles to work. Now she has a car herself, and has forgotten that old idea of **hers.** **30**

6. If you **practice** your English every day, instead of once a week, you will learn much more quickly. **39**

7. She practices the piano every afternoon, come hell or high water.

8. **What** do we call the two children's diseases that cover the victim with red spots? We call them measles and chickenpox. **28**

9. The general hat to **oversee** the movements of three divisions. **35**

10. If I **had not seen** the car coming and been able to jump aside, I would have been killed. **37**

11. He who doesn't have a chance to express himself is always frustrated.

12. They did not **want** him to make a mistake. **29**

13. He likes eating sugar cubes because he likes the way they crunch.

14. An early American pioneer woke up one morning with part of his beard gone because a curious mouse had nibbled some of it during the night.

15. It was terribly embarrassing to discover that I had no money in my pocket to pay the bill at the restaurant. Such a thing **had never happened** to me before. **31**

Übung 22

1. My host of the previous evening asked me if my wife and I got home safe and sound.

2. Beauty is in the eye of the beholder, they say.

3. Hoping someone would give him some money, the guitar player set his hat on the ground in front of himself.

4. Sucking your thumb when you're small is not a bad thing, if it gives you extra security.

5. I brought her to the edge of the cliff to see the view.

6. I am used to drive fast, but I don't have any accidents in spite of my speeding, because I know how to handle my car.

7. Upon entering a church I always feel less hurried.

8. Telling the truth may be noble, but it isn't fun.

9. An always greater variety of goods on the shelves of shops is usually a sign that the country is prosperous.

10. The accident occurred while I crossed the street.

11. People who come too late to church disturb the people who come on time.

12. The young man was up to his ears in debt because he didn't like to accept help from his father.

13. It is impossible for one supervisor to overlook the work of more than twenty workers.

14. It was a characteristic of him to always remain cool as a cucumber.

15. Too many suggestions and no help can drive you crazy.

Lösung 22

1. My host of the previous evening asked me if my wife and I **had got** home safe and sound. **31**

2. Beauty is in the eye of the beholder, they say.

3. Hoping someone would give him some money, the guitar player set his hat on the ground in front of himself.

4. Sucking your thumb when you're small is not a bad thing, if it gives you extra security.

5. I **took** her to the edge of the cliff to see the view. **32**

6. I am used to **driving** fast, but I don't have any accidents in spite of my speeding, because I know how to handle my car. **38**

7. Upon entering a church I always feel less hurried.

8. Telling the truth may be noble, but it isn't fun.

9. An **ever** greater variety of goods on the shelves of shops is usually a sign that the country is prosperous. **26**

10. The accident occurred while I **was crossing** the street. **36**

11. People who come **late** to church disturb the people who come on time. **33**

12. The young man was up to his ears in debt because he didn't **want** to accept help from his father. **29**

13. It is impossible for one supervisor to **oversee** the work of more than twenty workers. **35**

14. It was a characteristic of **his** to always remain cool as a cucumber. **30**

15. Too many suggestions and no help can drive you crazy.

Übung 23

1. During my holidays I stood at the seaside.

2. The table whose leg is broken is made of imported walnut.

3. If you will do your exercises every day, you will soon see for yourself how much fun it is to be able to speak a foreign language.

4. It took us five hours to clean up the mess he and his guests had left in our living room.

5. Staying with friends is fun for a while, but gets tiring if you have to change your life style to suit theirs.

6. A giraffe with a sore throat is a sorry sight.

7. The executive is used to make quick decisions.

8. Wives don't like their husbands to overlook how they run the household; they don't like being supervised.

9. The idea came to me, believe it or not, while I took a bath with my rubber duck!

10. Why are you eating so quickly? Because I like to get finished.

11. The messenger brought her a telegram containing only bad news.

12. Waiter, I become a beefsteak, please!

13. The investigation showed the airplane was not checked properly before the fatal flight.

14. Their hobbies are the same as ours: collecting stamps and collecting paintings by the great Impressionists.

15. If your teacher refuses to leave the classroom while all of you are in it, she must believe that all hell will break loose the moment her back is turned.

Lösung 23

1. During my holidays I **stayed** at the seaside. **40**

2. The table whose leg is broken is made of imported walnut. **41**

3. If you **do** your exercises every day, you will soon see for yourself how much fun it is to be able to speak a foreign language. **37**

4. It took us five hours to clean up the mess he and his guests had left in our living room.

5. Staying with friends is fun for a while, but gets tiring if you have to change your life style to suit theirs.

6. A giraffe with a sore throat is a sorry sight.

7. The executive is used to **making** quick decisions. **38**

8. Wives don't like their husbands to **oversee** how they run the household; they don't like being supervised. **35**

9. The idea came to me, believe it or not, while I **was taking** a bath with my rubber duck! **36**

10. Why are you eating so quickly? Because I **want** to get finished. **29**

11. The messenger **took** her a telegram containing only bad news. **32**

12. Waiter, I **get** a beefsteak, please! **42**

13. The investigation showed that the airplane **had not been** checked properly before the fatal flight. **31**

14. Their hobbies are the same as ours: collecting stamps and collecting paintings by the great Impressionists.

15. If your teacher refuses to leave the classroom while all of you are in it, she must believe that all hell will break loose the moment her back is turned.

Übung 24

1. I stood in the house all day, waiting for him to call.

2. The bank robber was hit by the policeman's bullet while he ran down the street.

3. It was a policy of them never to give credit, but we usually do.

4. If you want to become a really good golfer it is not enough to train your golf only on the weekend.

5. The policeman stopped the traffic and brought the old lady safely across the street.

6. Did you make any mistakes when you did your homework?

7. A nurse at a big hospital must be used to see a lot of blood.

8. I ate too much, and now I'm sick.

9. She apologized for arriving 45 minutes too late.

10. If you will go to the theatre tonight, you will see a wonderful play.

11. He bought a new coffee machine for the office, but because it broke the first week he had it, he felt he hadn't been lucky in this purchase.

12. Degrees and titles should not be so important as they are.

13. I'm completely fed up with your nonsense, so shape up or ship out!

14. The president of the meeting jumped up from his chair so quickly that he spilled his water and broke the glass. He apologized, blushed, and sat down again.

15. The splitting of Korea into two parts is the same like the splitting of Germany.

Lösung 24

1. I **stayed** in the house all day, waiting for him to call. **40**

2. The bank robber was hit by the policeman's bullet while he **was running** down the street. **36**

3. It was a policy of **theirs** never to give credit, but we usually do. **30**

4. If you want to become a really good golfer it is not enough to **practice** your golf only on the weekend. **39**

5. The policeman stopped the traffic and **took** the old lady safely across the street. **32**

6. Did you make any mistakes when you did your homework?

7. A nurse at a big hospital must be used to **seeing** a lot of blood. **38**

8. I ate too much, and now I'm sick.

9. She apologized for arriving 45 minutes **late.** **33**

10. If you **go** to the theatre tonight, you will see a wonderful play. **37**

11. He bought a new coffee machine for the office, but because it broke the first week he had it, he felt he hadn't been lucky in this purchase.

12. Degrees and titles should not be so important as they are.

13. I'm completely fed up with your nonsense, so shape up or ship out!

14. The president of the meeting jumped up from his chair so quickly that he spilled his water and broke the glass. He apologized, blushed, and sat down again.

15. The splitting of Korea into two parts is **like** (or) **the same as** the splitting of Germany. **43**

Übung 25

1. He said we should all love one another. I think so, too, but sometimes it's awfully difficult.

2. Never go anywhere on the thirteenth of a month if it's a Friday. It's unlucky.

3. While I rowed the boat toward the shore it began to sink.

4. The man who left the table before the dessert was served missed the best part of the meal.

5. After a while, the new-comers must be able to do the same work like the old-timers.

6. If the girl continues to train the piano as much as she has up till now, she is bound to learn to play well.

7. This book, whose cover is dirty and torn, is not inexpensive, for it is a rare book. I've been searching for it for three months, and until now I have not seen it anywhere.

8. To repair the kitchen cupboard, he had to take it off the wall.

9. He was up until five o'clock in the morning writing letters.

10. Her teeth were so strong she could take bottle caps off with them!

11. The pioneer woman killed rats with her pitchfork.

12. I want to become a degree in philosophy.

13. Do you like hard or soft boiled eggs for breakfast?

14. We stood at a hotel the first week we were here, and our money disappeared rapidly because of it.

15. If I would only have stayed a little longer, I would have succeeded in persuading her to marry me.

Lösung 25

1. He said we should all love one another. I think so, too, but sometimes it's awfully difficult.

2. Never go anywhere on the thirteenth of a month if it's a Friday. It's unlucky.

3. While I **was rowing** the boat toward the shore it began to sink. **36**

4. The man who **had left** the table before the dessert was served missed the best part of the meal. **31**

5. After a while, the new-comers must be able to do the same work **as** the old-timers. **43**

6. If the girl continues to **practice** the piano as much as she has up till now, she is bound to learn to play well. **39**

7. This book, whose cover is dirty and torn, is not inexpensive, for it is a rare book. I've been searching for it for three months, and until now I have not seen it anywhere. **41**

8. To repair the kitchen cupboard, he had to take it off the wall.

9. He was up until five o'clock in the morning writing letters.

10. Her teeth were so strong she could take bottle caps off with them!

11. The pioneer woman killed rats with her pitchfork.

12. I want to **get** a degree in philosophy. **42**

13. Do you like hard or soft boiled eggs for breakfast?

14. We **stayed** at a hotel the first week we were here, and our money disappeared rapidly because of it. **40**

15. If I **had only stayed** a little longer, I would have succeeded in persuading her to marry me. **37**

Übung 26

1. A pilot who must fly to London regularly must get used to make instrument landings because of the heavy fog.

2. They called their twin sons Pete and Repeat.

3. Most tennis coaches are usually not professionals, but simply people who have trained their tennis so much that they have become good enough to show others how to play.

4. Which is a better cure for a cold, vitamin "C," or hot and cold showers?

5. The embassy received a package whose explosive contents destroyed a whole street-full of buildings.

6. The least you can do to help me is make a little less noise!

7. At no other place does life pulse more hectically than in New York.

8. He shone his shoes yesterday.

9. The troubles that you have had are the same like those I've had.

10. Sometimes children have to be told "no."

11. She ever hoped she could become a movie star, but she never succeeded.

12. If every person would act exactly as he liked, life would be a pretty chaotic affair.

13. They stood at the party for hours because they didn't want to go back home.

14. On Saturday I hope to go to the pet shop and become a parakeet.

15. When asked by the salesman if he might buy a new car, the man answered that he was interesting.

Lösung 26

1. A pilot who must fly to London regularly must get used to **making** instrument landings because of the heavy fog. **38**

2. They called their twin sons Pete and Repeat.

3. Most tennis coaches are usually not professionals, but simply people who have **practiced** their tennis so much that they have become good enough to show others how to play. **39**

4. Which is a better cure for a cold, vitamin "C," or hot and cold showers?

5. The embassy received a package whose explosive contents destroyed a whole street-full of buildings. **41**

6. The least you can do to help me is make a little less noise!

7. At no other place does life pulse more hectically than in New York. **44**

8. He **shined** his shoes yesterday. **34**

9. The troubles that you have had are **like** those I've had. **43**

10. Sometimes children have to be told "no."

11. She **always** hoped she could become a movie star, but she never succeeded. **26**

12. If every person **acted** exactly as he liked, life would be a pretty chaotic affair. **37**

13. They **stayed** at the party for hours because they didn't want to go back home. **40**

14. On Saturday I hope to go the pet shop and **get** a parakeet. **42**

15. When asked by the salesman if he might buy a new car, the man answered that he was **interested.** **45**

Übung 27

1. The new assistant was told not to overlook the work of his subordinates too carefully during his first few weeks on the job.

2. The typical member of an Olympic team trains his sport six hours a day.

3. If children would take the advice of their parents more often, they would be spared many a headache later on in life.

4. Since my husband deserted me, and your husband deserted you, we're in the same boat.

5. Living in New York in August is the same like living in the tropics.

6. When asked if he wanted the firm to send him their prospectus in order to supply him with more information, the prospective customer answered that he was not interesting.

7. My house is in the near of the bakery.

8. My principle was and is to get whatever work is on my desk finished before leaving the office.

9. Last year I lay on the beach all summer and got a beautiful tan.

10. She shone the furniture with a cloth.

11. In spite of his many years on the bench, the judge was never able to get used to deal with women who suddenly burst into tears.

12. He will become a better position in the firm next year.

13. Do you coax your husband or bully him, to make him do what you want?

14. My mother hates my new haircut.

15. Even though we told them to come home early, they stood at the restaurant until late.

Lösung 27

1. The new assistant was told not to **oversee** the work of his subordinates too carefully during his first few weeks on the job. **35**

2. The typical member of an Olympic team **practices** his sport six hours a day. **39**

3. If children **took** the advice of their parents more often, they would be spared many a headache later on in life. **37**

4. Since my husband deserted me, and your husband deserted you, we're in the same boat.

5. Living in New York in August is **like** living in the tropics. **43**

6. When asked if he wanted the firm to send him their prospectus in order to supply him with more information, the prospective customer answered that he was not **interested.** **45**

7. My house is **near** the bakery. **48**

8. My principle **has been** to get whatever work is on my desk finished before leaving the office. **46**

9. Last year I lay on the beach all summer and got a beautiful tan. **47**

10. She **shined** the furniture with a cloth. **34**

11. In spite of his many years on the bench, the judge was never able to get used to **dealing** with women who suddenly burst into tears. **38**

12. He will **get** a better position in the firm next year. **42**

13. Do you coax your husband or bully him, to make him do what you want?

14. My mother hates my new haircut.

15. Even though we told them to come home early, they **stayed** at the restaurant until late. **40**

Übung 28

1. Seldom do statistics tell anyone much, and they are often completely useless.

2. The man was so tired that he did not hear the alarm clock. He lay in bed until his wife finally shook him awake.

3. To get rich today is just as difficult like one hundred years ago.

4. He took one look at his date and turned and ran because she was so ugly.

5. A great violinist once said, "A violinist must train every day. If I don't train for one day, I notice the difference. If I don't train for two days, my wife notices it; and if I don't train for three days, the critics notice it."

6. The window washer shone the windows.

7. When asked if she wanted to book the round-the-world voyage, the woman replied that she was interesting, but that she had not yet made up her mind.

8. Our pizza was so salty we couldn't eat it, but we drank a lot of beer.

9. He can cook one hundred different dishes without looking at a recipe.

10. I must become a new broom or the floor will always be dirty.

11. When I was eight years old I had a horse.

12. The little boy, thinking nervously about his mother's anger, was anxious to get dirty.

13. They demolished the old building to make room for a new one.

14. I want that he says what he thinks.

15. When you go shopping today, will you be in the near of a flower shop?

Lösung 28

1. Seldom do statistics tell anyone much, and they are often completely useless. **44**

2. The man was so tired that he did not hear the alarm clock. He lay in bed until his wife finally shook him awake. **47**

3. To get rich today is just as difficult **as** one hundred years ago. **43**

4. He took one look at his date and turned and ran because she was so ugly.

5. A great violinist once said, "A violinist must **practice** every day. If I don't **practice** for one day, I notice the difference. If I don't **practice** for two days, my wife notices it; and if I don't **practice** for three days, the critics notice it." **39**

6. The window washer **shined** the windows. **34**

7. When asked if she wanted to book the round-the-world voyage, the woman replied that she was **interested,** but that she had not yet made up her mind. **45**

8. Our pizza was so salty we couldn't eat it, but we drank a lot of beer.

9. He can cook one hundred different dishes without looking at a recipe.

10. I must **get** a new broom or the floor will always be dirty. **42**

11. When I was eight years old I had a horse.

12. The little boy, thinking nervously about his mother's anger, was anxious **about getting** dirty. **49**

13. They demolished the old building to make room for a new one.

14. I want **him to say** what he thinks. **50**

15. When you go shopping today, will you be **near** a flower shop? **48**

Übung 29

1. Today's women are not only interested in looking good; they want to have the same opportunity to develop and use their talents as men have.

2. The cleaning lady shone the mirrors.

3. They watched their neighbours through the window.

4. We tried to make potato chips, but it didn't work.

5. My family stood in Spain for a year when I was little.

6. If he becomes a new car, we must become one, too.

7. After living in the tropics for eight years and eating bananas every day, I wanted something else to eat.

8. He wants that we go where he's been.

9. What the bank robber wanted was the same like millions of honest people: money. But unlike millions of honest people, he was not willing to work for it.

10. Only when the wholesaler said that he would lower the price did the retailer say he was interesting.

11. Too many cooks spoil the broth.

12. Mr. Slough is tall, but his son is still taller than he.

13. She was anxious to go blind after she was hit in the eye by a stone.

14. Our television only works when we kick it.

15. If the river weren't so polluted we'd swim in it.

Lösung 29

1. Today's women are not only interested in looking good; they want to have the same opportunity to develop and use their talents as men have.

2. The cleaning lady **shined** the mirrors. **34**

3. They watched their neighbours through the window.

4. We tried to make potato chips, but it didn't work.

5. My family **stayed** in Spain for a year when I was little. **40**

6. If he **gets** a new car, we must **get** one, too. **42**

7. After living in the tropics for eight years and eating bananas every day, I wanted something else to eat.

8. He wants **us to go** where he's been. **50**

9. What the bank robber wanted was the same **as** millions of honest people: money. But unlike millions of honest people, he was not willing to work for it. **43**

10. Only when the wholesaler said that he would lower the price did the retailer say he was **interested.** **45**

11. Too many cooks spoil the broth.

12. Mr. Slough is tall, but his son is **even** taller than he. **51**

13. She was anxious **about going** blind after she was hit in the eye by a stone. **49**

14. Our television only works when we kick it.

15. If the river weren't so polluted we'd swim in it.

Übung 30

1. He always parks in the near of the bank.

2. He was ever eating chocolate. What a mistake! Besides being bad for his teeth, it made him fatter and fatter.

3. The Norwegians are a seafaring people for generations.

4. My ex-boss seemed to consider me as a kind of slave whom he could even call up at midnight if necessary.

5. The little boy shone the floor with his best handkerchief.

6. Because the woman wanted new living room furniture, she said she was interesting when a furniture salesman called her.

7. My little sister must have vanilla ice cream instead of chocolate so the drips and spills don't stain her clothes.

8. After his remarriage, he remarked: "Getting used to your new wife is just as difficult like getting rid of your old one."

9. Her car is big, but her fiancé's car is still bigger. His goes "Rrrrumm" and hers goes "Putt-putt-putt."

10. He has been studying medicine for the last five years.

11. We were anxious to make our host angry. We had to be careful of what we said to him, because he had a low boiling point.

12. I like him as a person, but when he is not successful he must leave the firm.

13. Since it didn't seem to make any difference to him whether she stayed or not, she left.

14. My mother is an exercise fanatic. Every morning she runs two miles.

15. Buying in large quantities often saves you money in the end.

Lösung 30

1. He always parks **near** the bank. **48**

2. He was **always** eating chocolate. What a mistake! Besides being bad for his teeth, it made him fatter and fatter. **26**

3. The Norwegians **have been** a seafaring people for generations. **46**

4. My ex-boss seemed to **consider me to be** a kind of slave whom he could even call up at midnight if necessary. **52**

5. The little boy **shined** the floor with his best handkerchief. **34**

6. Because the woman wanted new living room furniture, she said she was **interested** when a furniture salesman called her. **45**

7. My little sister must have vanilla ice cream instead of chocolate so the drips and spills don't stain her clothes.

8. After his remarriage, he remarked: "Getting used to your new wife is just as difficult **as** getting rid of your old one." **43**

9. Her car is big, but her fiancé's car is **even** bigger. His goes "Rrrrumm" and hers goes "Putt-putt-putt." **51**

10. He has been studying medicine for the last five years.

11. We were anxious **about making** our host angry. We had to be careful of what we said to him, because he had a low boiling point. **49**

12. I like him as a person, but **if** he is not successful he must leave the firm. **53**

13. Since it didn't seem to make any difference to him whether she stayed or not, she left. **54**

14. My mother is an exercise fanatic. Every morning she runs two miles.

15. Buying in large quantities often saves you money in the end.

Übung 31

1. He is considered as the best man we have.

2. Since it was impossible to find any fingerprints or other evidence, the police had to close the case.

3. You can tell from the look in his eye that he's lying.

4. We want that you are comfortable here.

5. That the product was sold at such a low price clearly indicated that the marketing firm was not interesting in promoting it.

6. The school is in the near of the park.

7. I was watching a man at the station yesterday while he shone the ticket machines.

8. Not all Americans chew gum constantly.

9. Pick the kitten you want to take with you. It doesn't make any difference to me which one you choose.

10. You should not forget that we are out of school for 15 years and are out of practice.

11. I am lucky to see that you have cut your hair at last!

12. My youngest daughter used to walk in her sleep and frighten the whole family.

13. "When you don't take that kitten back to where you found it, you will see what will happen!" the woman shouted at her children.

14. They say she is one of their most violent prisoners. Are you anxious to go into her prison cell alone?

15. They spent the afternoon on the balcony, watching the horses and sheep in the neighbouring field.

Lösung 31

1. He is **considered to be** the best man we have. **52**

2. Since it was impossible to find any fingerprints or other evidence, the police had to close the case. **54**

3. You can tell from the look in his eye that he's lying.

4. We want **you to be** comfortable here. **50**

5. That the product was sold at such a low price clearly indicated that the marketing firm was not **interested** in promoting it. **45**

6. The school is **near** the park. **48**

7. I was watching a man at the station yesterday while he **shined** the ticket machines. **34**

8. Not all Americans chew gum constantly.

9. Pick the kitten you want to take with you. It doesn't make any difference to me which one you choose.

10. You should not forget that we **have been** out of school for 15 years and are out of practice. **46**

11. I am **happy** to see that you have cut your hair at last! **55**

12. My youngest daughter used to walk in her sleep and frighten the whole family.

13. "**If** you don't take that kitten back to where you found it, you will see what will happen!" the woman shouted at her children. **53**

14. They say she is one of their most violent prisoners. Are you anxious **about going** into her prison cell alone? **49**

15. They spent the afternoon on the balcony, watching the horses and sheep in the neighbouring field.

Übung 32

1. It is difficult to speak well when your mouth is full of cookies.

2. I am not in Hamburg for 20 years and must admit that things have changed considerably since I was last here.

3. The child closed his eyes and opened his mouth. We knew he would begin to scream in less than a second.

4. I've only been to England once, but he has been there seven times.

5. Some consider it as feminine for a man to mind the baby.

6. Listening to good music sends me to sleep.

7. Once you get the reputation of being a troublemaker, people continually accuse you of starting fights that you didn't start.

8. A house whose walls are not insulated sufficiently is not only noisy, but much more expensive to heat.

9. It was a very stormy romance, but when she asked him when they would get married, she found out that he was not interesting.

10. When it does not stop raining soon I will be in trouble because I must leave for my appointment in a few minutes.

11. Treat him gently. He's already on pins and needles about his coming interview with the boss and doesn't need any more exitement.

12. I arrived late because I had taken the wrong train.

13. In this book it says that African elephants are different from Indian elephants.

14. If you don't like spaghetti, we want that you say so.

15. Why on earth did you throw away your baby book? The photos of you as a toddler were cute!

Lösung 32

1. It is difficult to speak well when your mouth is full of cookies.

2. I **have not been** in Hamburg for 20 years and must admit that things have changed considerably since I was last here. **46**

3. The child closed his eyes and opened his mouth! We knew he would begin to scream in less than a second.

4. I've only been to England once, but he has been there seven times.

5. Some consider it **to be** feminine for a man to mind the baby. **52**

6. Listening to good music sends me to sleep.

7. Once you get the reputation of being a troublemaker, people continually accuse you of starting fights that you didn't start.

8. A house whose walls are not insulated sufficiently is not only noisy, but much more expensive to heat. **41**

9. It was a very stormy romance, but when she asked him when they would get married, she found out that he was not **interested.** **45**

10. **If** it does not stop raining soon I will be in trouble because I must leave for my appointment in a few minutes. **53**

11. Treat him gently. He's already on pins and needles about his coming interview with the boss and doesn't need any more excitement.

12. I arrived late because I had taken the wrong train.

13. In this book it says that African elephants are different from Indian elephants.

14. If you don't like spaghetti, we want **you to say** so. **50**

15. Why on earth did you throw away your baby book? The photos of you as a toddler were cute!

Übung 33

1. "I am not in my office for two minutes and my telephone is already ringing," the businessman complains.

2. I have finally got used to not eating dinner.

3. Although he had never driven a car before, he was perfectly sure he could do it.

4. When someone broke his window, he filled the crack with newspapers.

5. She shone the table even though I had asked her not to.

6. In 1920 more people understood how to live well as today.

7. You may be tired but I am still more tired!

8. It is considered as a sign of good upbringing to dress properly for every occasion.

9. At the age of thirteen, she was still a tomboy playing football with her brothers, and refusing to wear dresses.

10. What he did was forbidden.

11. If you fight all the time, maybe you are tired.

12. They were anxious to fail.

13. Motor-boats scared her because they made so much noise.

14. Only if you listen to the teacher will you learn English.

15. There are some works to be done.

Lösung 33

1. "I **have not been** in my office for two minutes and my telephone is already ringing," the businessman complains. **46**

2. I have finally got used to not eating dinner.

3. Although he had never driven a car before, he was perfectly sure he could do it.

4. When someone broke his window, he filled the crack with newspapers.

5. She **shined** the table even though I had asked her not to. **34**

6. In 1920 more people understood how to live well **than** today. **56**

7. You may be tired but I am **even** more tired! **51**

8. It is considered **to be** a sign of good upbringing to dress properly for every occasion. **52**

9. At the age of thirteen, she was still a tomboy playing football with her brothers, and refusing to wear dresses.

10. What he did was forbidden. **57**

11. If you fight all the time, maybe you are tired.

12. They were anxious **about failing.** **49**

13. Motor-boats scared her because they made so much noise.

14. Only if you listen to the teacher will you learn English. **44**

15. There **is** some **work** to be done. **58**

Übung 34

1. He has more money as I. That's why he lives so much better.

2. "The weather is not good since we came," the vacationers complained. They are determined to take out an insurance policy against this risk next year.

3. The accident victim lay in the street until someone saw him and called an ambulance.

4. Will it bother you if I play the piano?

5. He wants that everything pleases her.

6. Why is it that whenever one is lucky about something, something happens to ruin it?

7. "When you are not gone in one minute I will call the police!" the angry bartender told the drunk.

8. We caught sight of him in the near of the town hall.

9. After work she canned and froze her garden vegetables. By 9 p.m. she was exhausted.

10. The woman really had dark hairs, but had bleached them blond.

11. If you look for the information there, you'll never find it. You have to get it straight from the horse's mouth.

12. Caruso is considered as the world's greatest tenor.

13. If you don't ask questions, you'll never learn anything.

14. Sitting in the sun too long is bad for your skin.

15. To be efficient you must organize your time.

Lösung 34

1. He has more money **than** I. That's why he lives so much better. **56**

2. "The weather **has not been** good since we came," the vacationers complained. They are determined to take out an insurance policy against this risk next year. **46**

3. The accident victim lay in the street until someone saw him and called an ambulance. **47**

4. Will it bother you if I play the piano?

5. He wants **everything to please** her. **50**

6. Why is it that whenever one is **happy** about something, something happens to ruin it? **55**

7. "**If** you are not gone in one minute I will call the police!" the angry bartender told the drunk. **53**

8. We caught sight of him **near** the town hall. **48**

9. After work she canned and froze her garden vegetables. By 9 p.m. she was exhausted.

10. The woman really had dark **hair,** but had bleached **it** blond. **58**

11. If you look for the information there, you'll never find it. You have to get it straight from the horse's mouth.

12. Caruso is considered **to be** the world's greatest tenor. **52**

13. If you don't ask questions, you'll never learn anything.

14. Sitting in the sun too long is bad for your skin.

15. To be efficient you must organize your time.

Übung 35

1. The small child hated stairs because he was anxious to fall down.

2. The cat was so interested in chasing the mouse that it forgot it was too big to run under the sofa, and banged its head against it as the mouse escaped.

3. Taking the time to make friends now will be valuable later.

4. You must be blind as a bat not to see that she's as poor as a church-mouse!

5. Rarely will you find a man who cannot be swayed by a woman.

6. There were three goldfishes in the bowl.

7. It is easier to learn one foreign language after the other, as to learn two at the same time.

8. If a man refuses to do a dirty job he has right.

9. The stray dog, whose owner did not pick it up at the dogpound, was given to an old lady.

10. He told him that his friend had left ten minutes ago.

11. I consider him as a very intelligent person.

12. He was not lucky about his wife's running away with another man.

13. The tired businessman lay in the bathtub of his hotel room and soaked away the problems of the day.

14. He was shaken to the roots by his discovery of a corpse in his closet.

15. How early should you start training your child to be neat? While he's still young, during his fourth year, I believe.

Lösung 35

1. The small child hated stairs because he was anxious **about falling** down. **49**

2. The cat was so interested in chasing the mouse that it forgot it was too big to run under the sofa, and banged its head against it as the mouse escaped.

3. Taking the time to make friends now will be valuable later.

4. You must be blind as a bat not to see that she's as poor as a church-mouse!

5. Rarely will you find a man who cannot be swayed by a woman. **44**

6. There were three **goldfish** in the bowl. **58**

7. It is easier to learn one foreign language after the other, **than** to learn two at the same time. **56**

8. If a man refuses to do a dirty job he **is** right. **59**

9. The stray dog, whose owner did not pick it up at the dogpound, was given to an old lady. **41**

10. He told him that his friend had left ten minutes **before.** **60**

11. I consider him **to be** a very intelligent person. **52**

12. He was not **happy** about his wife's running away with another man. **55**

13. The tired businessman lay in the bathtub of his hotel room and soaked away the problems of the day. **47**

14. He was shaken to the roots by his discovery of a corpse in his closet.

15. How early should you start training your child to be neat? While he's still young, during his fourth year, I believe.

Übung 36

1. If it seems crazy to you too, he wants that you tell him so.

2. They met in the near of the zoo.

3. Because there were discrepancies in the informations they received, they couldn't form a clear picture of what had happened.

4. Martin Luther King had right when he said that everyone had to have the right to vote no matter what the color of his skin.

5. "When you want me to answer your question about where I was all night, you must let me speak!" the man shouted at his furious wife.

6. The woman who had been hypnotized lay in a trance until the hypnotist snapped his fingers.

7. The hats of the gentlemen are black.

8. A friend is someone who is sad when you are sad, and lucky when you are lucky.

9. If you want to arrive anywhere on time you must leave on time.

10. A car whose motor is not adjusted properly will consume much too much fuel.

11. By the time he was 80, he had a mattress full of money, but he never spent any of it.

12. The director explained that the company had experienced its greatest postwar financial crisis only six months ago.

13. The Germans have a saying that goes: "It is better to be rich and healthy as poor and ill."

14. I like to hear people singing or whistling when they're happy.

15. Too often we jump to conclusions about people we don't know well.

Lösung 36

1. If it seems crazy to you too, he **wants you to tell** him so. **50**

2. They met **near** the zoo. **48**

3. Because there were discrepancies in the **information** they received, they couldn't form a clear picture of what had happened. **58**

4. Martin Luther King **was** right when he said that everyone had to have the right to vote no matter what the color of his skin. **59**

5. "**If** you want me to answer your question about where I was all night, you must let me speak!" the man shouted at his furious wife. **53**

6. The woman who had been hypnotized lay in a trance until the hypnotist snapped his fingers. **47**

7. The **gentlemen's** hats are black. **61**

8. A friend is someone who is sad when you are sad, and **happy** when you are **happy.** **55**

9. If you want to arrive anywhere on time you must leave on time. **62**

10. A car whose motor is not adjusted properly will consume much too much fuel. **41**

11. By the time he was 80, he had a mattress full of money, but he never spent any of it.

12. The director explained that the company had experienced its greatest postwar financial crisis only six months **before.** **60**

13. The Germans have a saying that goes: "It is better to be rich and healthy **than** poor and ill." **56**

14. I like to hear people singing or whistling when they're happy.

15. Too often we jump to conclusions about people we don't know well.

Übung 37

1. The ideas of the men are good, but this is not the kind of problem that can be solved by a committee.

2. When you don't want to catch a cold you must dress more warmly.

3. My grandfather collects silver dollars.

4. He had right to say no to that request because it was unfair.

5. I don't know why you are so lucky. You have just lost every penny you ever earned.

6. The more clothes she buys, the more she wants.

7. Is a woman more emotional as a man?

8. The lady had an apartment on Fifth Avenue. Her maid had an apartment that was on Third Avenue.

9. The woman told her lawyer that she had proof that her husband had run away with another woman three months ago.

10. He did not get the reply on the day he needed it because the mail had not come on time.

11. If we change our plans and then don't tell Kevin, it will be hitting him below the belt.

12. The man's watch lay on the restaurant table for four hours until he returned and found it exactly where he had left it. He had had luck.

13. My husband is sick, but I'm still sicker.

14. An encyclopedia attempts to accumulate and present in easily accessible form the knowledges of many centuries.

15. It would be a very good idea for all of us to teach another.

Lösung 37

1. The **men's ideas** are good, but this is not the kind of problem that can be solved by a committee. **61**

2. **If** you don't want to catch a cold you must dress more warmly. **53**

3. My grandfather collects silver dollars.

4. He **was** right to say no to that request because it was unfair. **59**

5. I don't know why you are so **happy.** You have just lost every penny you ever earned. **55**

6. The more clothes she buys, the more she wants.

7. Is a woman more emotional **than** a man? **56**

8. The lady had an apartment on Fifth Avenue. Her maid had an apartment that was on Third Avenue. **57**

9. The woman told her lawyer that she had proof that her husband had run away with another woman three months **before.** **60**

10. He did not get the reply on the day he needed it because the mail had not come on time. **62**

11. If we change our plans and then don't tell Kevin, it will be hitting him below the belt.

12. The man's watch lay on the restaurant table for four hours until he returned and found it exactly where he had left it. He had had luck. **47**

13. My husband is sick, but I'm **even** sicker. 51

14. An encyclopedia attempts to accumulate and present in easily accessible form the **knowledge** of many centuries. **58**

15. It would be a very good idea for all of us to teach **one another.** **63**

Übung 38

1. She is not possible to do the work.

2. High humidity causes bread to mold.

3. It is a major disaster for the television to break on Friday evening.

4. Has the new restaurant opened yet? Yes, I think.

5. If he won more tennis matches as I it was only because he cheated. In reality I am the better player.

6. Only when he earnestly began to listen to others' opinions did he become more tolerant.

7. He told his acquaintance that he had first visited Rome seven years ago.

8. I told him that I was not interested in anything he had to say.

9. The parents were not lucky about the bad grades their children had brought home from school.

10. Her book is thick, but my sister's is still thicker than hers.

11. We have right when we ask you to respect others.

12. The eyes of the woman are a shade of blue the likes of which you have never seen before.

13. When I have nightmares, I sleep badly.

14. Sit still, David, and stop wiggling.

15. They toasted marshmallows in the fireplace.

Lösung 38

1. She is not **able** to do the work. **64**

2. High humidity causes bread to mold.

3. It is a major disaster for the television to break on Friday evening.

4. Has the new restaurant opened yet? Yes, I think **so.** **65**

5. If he won more tennis matches **than** I it was only because he cheated. In reality I am the better player. **56**

6. Only when he earnestly began to listen to others' opinions did he become more tolerant. **44**

7. He told his acquaintance that he had first visited Rome seven years **before.** **60**

8. I told him that I was not interested in anything he had to say. **57**

9. The parents were not **happy** about the bad grades their children had brought home from school. **55**

10. Her book is thick, but my sister's is **even** thicker than hers. **51**

11. We **are** right when we ask you to respect others. **59**

12. The **woman's** eyes are a shade of blue the likes of which you have never seen before. **61**

13. When I have nightmares, I sleep badly.

14. Sit still, David, and stop wiggling.

15. They toasted marshmallows in the fireplace.

Übung 39

1. If you are thirty-five years old and not possible to walk upstairs without panting, then you are in bad physical condition.

2. I have a radio in the kitchen which I can switch on whenever I want it.

3. He flew into a rage when she told him to stop smoking.

4. Her job was to clean the bathroom every week.

5. The sun has finally come out and the sky is clearing.

6. Since the woman lived alone in a little room and never went out or had visitors, everyone pitied her. No one realized how rich she was.

7. If you like fish, you'll love lobster!

8. The child sat alone on the subway seat, swinging his legs and singing to himself.

9. We have not seen another for twenty years.

10. Lunch at the hotel was served from twelve till two. If you were not there on time, you had to be satisfied with left-overs.

11. Seldom did William Faulkner write about anywhere but the U.S. South.

12. That what I wanted to say but could not because you interrupted, was that you were right.

13. Their child is smart, but my brother was still smarter than he at the age of six.

14. On long winter evenings he cut out paper dolls to amuse his daughter.

15. Parents have always right.

Lösung 39

1. If you are thirty-five years old and not **able** to walk upstairs without panting, then you are in bad physical condition. **64**

2. I have a radio in the kitchen which I can switch on whenever I want **to.** **65**

3. He flew into a rage when she told him to stop smoking.

4. Her job was to clean the bathroom every week.

5. The sun has finally come out and the sky is clearing.

6. Since the woman lived alone in a little room and never went out or had visitors, everyone pitied her. No one realized how rich she was. **54**

7. If you like fish, you'll love lobster!

8. The child sat alone on the subway seat, swinging his legs and singing to himself.

9. We have not seen **each other** for twenty years. **63**

10. Lunch at the hotel was served from twelve till two. If you were not there on time, you had to be satisfied with left-overs. **62**

11. Seldom did William Faulkner write about anywhere but the U.S. South. **44**

12. **What** I wanted to say but could not because you interrupted, was that you were right. **66**

13. Their child is smart, but my brother was **even** smarter than he at the age of six. **51**

14. On long winter evenings he cut out paper dolls to amuse his daughter.

15. Parents **are** always right. **59**

1. It was understood by all present that the situation was a completely different one from that of five years ago.

2. The lady leaned so far over her balcony railing that she fell over, much to the surprise of the people below.

3. He said her that the food was cold.

4. Is he happy here? Yes, I think.

5. I am anxious about winding my watch for fear the winder may break. It has often broken before.

6. The employee was finally fired because he never came to work on time.

7. The cat stepped carefully across the wet roof.

8. The social worker tried to make it clear to the young boy that it was not good to steal.

9. They greeted another warmly.

10. The sailor told a very interesting story, but that what he said he had done was simply impossible.

11. Unpaved roads make driving slow, as do detours.

12. The teacher has right when she tells you to practice.

13. There are people who are not possible to control themselves when something angers them. I am one of those people.

14. You had better have a dentist check that bad tooth of yours.

15. The man felt unhappy because he saw that some of the things he had said had been misinterpreted by his acquaintances.

Lösung 40

1. It was understood by all present that the situation was a completely different one from that of five years **before.** **60**

2. The lady leaned so far over her balcony railing, that she fell over, much to the surprise of the people below.

3. He **told** her that the food was cold. **67**

4. Is he happy here? Yes, I think **so.** **65**

5. I am anxious about winding my watch for fear the winder may break. It has often broken before.

6. The employee was finally fired because he never came to work on time. **62**

7. The cat stepped carefully across the wet roof.

8. The social worker tried to make it clear to the young boy that it was not good to steal. **57**

9. They greeted **each other** warmly. **63**

10. The sailor told a very interesting story, but **what** he said he had done was simply impossible. **66**

11. Unpaved roads make driving slow, as do detours.

12. The teacher **is** right when she tells you to practice. **59**

13. There are people who are not **able** to control themselves when something angers them. I am one of those people. **64**

14. You had better have a dentist check that bad tooth of yours.

15. The man felt unhappy because he saw that some of the things he had said had been misinterpreted by his acquaintances.

Übung 41

1. If you said him that you would be at his home by 9 a.m., you should have been there at that time.

2. She spends hours gazing into the mirror and admiring herself, which is a bit odd since she isn't pretty any more.

3. The professor explained that a repetition of what had occurred three years ago was not possible under contemporary conditions.

4. The group of little boys found a dead rat in the street. The boys looked at it and saw that it had lost its tail.

5. We are good friends. We write another often.

6. The majority of the people were for him.

7. The old farmer went on doing things the way he had always done them since he had no faith in the new methods of farming.

8. He declared that he had always felt fit as a fiddle and right as rain.

9. The building will be finished until spring.

10. It needs only five minutes to prepare a Chinese meal.

11. A person who is not possible to express himself well in words is not necessarily dumb.

12. Beggars upset me.

13. Since I only learned the name of the man this morning, it was impossible for me to get in contact with him.

14. My mother taught me that it was our duty to help those who were not so fortunate as we were.

15. Sometimes I like to get up early in the morning, or, as people sometimes say, at the crack of dawn.

Lösung 41

1. If you **told** him that you would be at his home by 9 a.m., you should have been there at that time. **67**

2. She spends hours gazing into the mirror and admiring herself, which is a bit odd since she isn't pretty any more.

3. The professor explained that a repetition of what had occurred three years **before** was not possible under contemporary conditions. **60**

4. The group of little boys found a dead rat in the street. The boys looked at it and saw that it had lost its tail.

5. We are good friends. We write **each other** often. **63**

6. The majority of the people **was** for him. **68**

7. The old farmer went on doing things the way he had always done them since he had no faith in the new methods of farming. **54**

8. He declared that he had always felt fit as a fiddle and right as rain.

9. The building will be finished **by** spring. **69**

10. It **takes** only five minutes to prepare a Chinese meal. **70**

11. A person who is not **able** to express himself well in words is not necessarily dumb. **64**

12. Beggars upset me.

13. Since I only learned the **man's name** this morning, it was impossible for me to get in contact with him. **61**

14. My mother taught me that it was our duty to help those who were not so fortunate as we were. **57**

15. Sometimes I like to get up early in the morning, or, as people sometimes say, at the crack of dawn.

Übung 42

1. Twenty-three per cent of the young men in the country are ill and therefore cannot be draftet into the army.

2. If you help me and I help you, we help another.

3. That what he did was illegal.

4. If I am not at your home until 7 p.m. please leave without me.

5. Either walk to the nearest gas station or hitchhike to the nearest garage. That's all what I can suggest.

6. The children of the widow were so badly behaved that they were thrown out of school.

7. Although it is very difficult to buy the correct thing for a man who has everything, a little present should enjoy him.

8. He isn't coming after all? But he said he wanted it!

9. Does eating peanuts make you thirsty? Yes, it always does.

10. The driver took the road that led to the right since the other road seemed too poor to use.

11. The toy store had a music box attached to the door that played a tune when people entered.

12. It needs only half an hour to reach the center of the city.

13. Two small girls with a doll carriage were standing at the bus stop, waiting with the adults.

14. The doctor did not say him the real nature of the illness because he knew the patient would not be able to bear the truth.

15. Her apartment was crowded with African plants and tropical fish. Her neighbours privately thought she was crazy, and I thought so, too!

Lösung 42

1. Twenty-three per cent of the young men in the country is ill and therefore cannot be drafted into the army. **68**

2. If you help me and I help you, we help **each other.** **63**

3. **What** he did was illegal. **66**

4. If I am not at your home **by** 7 p.m. please leave without me. **69**

5. Either walk to the nearest gas station or hitchhike to the nearest garage. That's all **that** I can suggest. **71**

6. The **widow's children** were so badly behaved that they were thrown out of school. **61**

7. Although it is very difficult to buy the correct thing for a man who has everything, a little present should **please** him. **72**

8. He isn't coming after all? But he said he wanted **to**! **65**

9. Does eating peanuts make you thirsty? Yes, it always does.

10. The driver took the road that led to the right since the other road seemed too poor to use. **54**

11. The toy store had a music box attached to the door that played a tune when people entered.

12. It **takes** only half an hour to reach the center of the city. **70**

13. Two small girls with a doll carriage were standing at the bus stop, waiting with the adults.

14. The doctor did not **tell** him the real nature of the illness because he knew the patient would not be able to bear the truth. **67**

15. Her apartment was crowded with African plants and tropical fish. Her neighbours privately thought she was crazy, and I thought so, too!

Übung 43

1. His deeds show that he doesn't care about all what he does.

2. Are you a vegetarian who won't eat eggs?

3. He told me that he must take his mother to the doctor because she felt ill.

4. It enjoys him that she likes his new suit.

5. It is only a question of time before the physical therapy the man is receiving will make him possible to overcome the physical handicap he suffered and resume a normal life.

6. I object to your not answering the question.

7. If we give him a higher salary he will be more likely to stay working for us than if we don't give him a raise.

8. When they first met another they were nervous. Later they got well acquainted and were relaxed when they were together.

9. Did he have a good reason for coming late? Yes, I think.

10. The upcoming celebration is for their twentieth wedding aniversary. It is going to take place in their own house.

11. If you want to succeed in school, set a date that you know you can keep to get the work done, and then hand it in on time.

12. Because the construction workers were driving piles just down the street, it was impossible to concentrate.

13. You have to repay the money until the 30th of March at the latest. After that date it will be too late.

14. The earnings of the famous jockey well exceeded one million dollars.

15. In my dictionary it says that this word comes from the Latin.

Lösung 43

1. His deeds show that he doesn't care about all **that** he does. **71**

2. Are you a vegetarian who won't eat eggs?

3. He told me that he **had to** take his mother to the doctor because she felt ill. **73**

4. It **pleases** him that she likes his new suit. **72**

5. It is only a question of time before the physical therapy the man is receiving will make him **able** to overcome the physical handicap he suffered and resume a normal life. **64**

6. I object to your not answering the question. **74**

7. If we give him a higher salary he will be more likely to **keep** working for us than if we don't give him a raise. **75**

8. When they first met **each other** they were nervous. Later they got well acquainted and were relaxed when they were together. **63**

9. Did he have a good reason for coming late? Yes, I think **so.** **65**

10. The upcoming celebration is for their twentieth wedding aniversary. It is going to take place in their own house.

11. If you want to succeed in school, set a date that you know you can keep to get the work done, and then hand it in on time. **62**

12. Because the construction workers were driving piles just down the street, it was impossible to concentrate.

13. You have to repay the money **by** the 30th of March at the latest. After that date it will be too late. **69**

14. The **famous jockey's earnings** well exceeded one million dollars. **61**

15. In my dictionary it says that this word comes from the Latin.

Übung 44

1. Yesterday I heard a woman tell her twenty-year-old daughter that she must be home by 11 p.m. that night.

2. A child who has no brothers or sisters is often fond of animals.

3. Why do you want to climb the tower? Just because I want it.

4. Pudding enjoys the old lady because she doesn't have to chew it.

5. To say you are sorry needs only one second, but may have results that last for years.

6. There are some people who say that a man who is possible to go to collect his unemployment cheque is also possible to work.

7. If I don't have a proposal of marriage from him until the end of the week, I will have to stop dating him and find someone else.

8. If you can play the piano well with long fingernails, I'll eat my hat!

9. It is the receptionist's duty to control whoever enters the building.

10. He'll stay telephoning until the world comes to an end if he doesn't get an answer.

11. If all what you need to succeed is the right idea, how do you explain the fact that so many intelligent people are poor?

12. We're looking forward to his visiting us.

13. Thirty-two per cent of all people killed in automobile accidents last year were under the influence of alcohol.

14. That what the politician had already said years before was now being proclaimed by the opposition as the only possible solution.

15. What you say depends from your point of view.

Lösung 44

1. Yesterday I heard a woman tell her twenty-year-old daughter that she **had to** be home by 11 p.m. that night. **73**

2. A child who has no brothers or sisters is often fond of animals.

3. Why do you want to climb the tower? Just because I want **to.** **65**

4. The old lady **likes** pudding because she doesn't have to chew it. **72**

5. To say you are sorry **takes** only one second, but may have results that last for years. **70**

6. There are some people who say that a man who is **able** to go to collect his unemployment cheque is also **able** to work. **64**

7. If I don't have a proposal of marriage from him **by** the end of the week, I will have to stop dating him and find someone else. **69**

8. If you can play the piano well with long fingernails, I'll eat my hat!

9. It is the receptionist's duty to **check** whoever enters the building. **76**

10. He'll **keep** telephoning until the world comes to an end if he doesn't get an answer. **75**

11. If all **that** you need to succeed is the right idea, how do you explain the fact that so many intelligent people are poor? **71**

12. We're looking forward to his visiting us. **74**

13. Thirty-two per cent of all people killed in automobile accidents last year **was** under the influence of alcohol. **68**

14. **What** the politician had already said years before was now being proclaimed by the opposition as the only possible solution. **66**

15. What you say depends **on** your point of view. **77**

Übung 45

1. Nobody understands me.

2. Whether you can take more than one holiday per year depends from how much money you have.

3. Until her husband was ready to give her what she wanted, she stayed bothering him.

4. They appreciated her helping them.

5. Seen from above, the earth looks round. From the ground, though, it appears to be flat.

6. It is unbelievable that he visited school for so long and still cannot speak English.

7. The fireman had to rescue the kitten that was stuck in a tree.

8. An old saying goes: "All what is necessary for evil to triumph is for good men to do nothing."

9. The doctor told his patient that he must come back for a check-up in three weeks.

10. A lonely person often talks too much when he finds himself with other people.

11. The librarian controls my bags as I leave the library.

12. I think she's right. He thinks, too.

13. I have heard it said that the most important man on board a ship is the cook, for if the meals aren't good, the ship loses its crew.

14. If Miss Brown is not back from her holidays until Friday or does not bother to inform us when she will return, we will fire her.

15. Your success enjoys me very much!

Lösung 45

1. Nobody understands me.

2. Whether you can take more than one holiday per year depends **on** how much money you have. **77**

3. Until her husband was ready to give her what she wanted, she **kept** bothering him. **75**

4. They appreciated her helping them. **74**

5. Seen from above, the earth looks round. From the ground, though, it appears to be flat.

6. It is unbelievable that he **attended** school for so long and still cannot speak English. **78**

7. The fireman had to rescue the kitten that was stuck in a tree.

8. An old saying goes: "All **that** is necessary for evil to triumph is for good men to do nothing." **71**

9. The doctor told his patient that he **had to** come back for a check-up in three weeks. **73**

10. A lonely person often talks too much when he finds himself with other people.

11. The librarian **checks** my bags as I leave the library. **76**

12. I think she's right. He thinks **so,** too. **65**

13. I have heard it said that the most important man on board a ship is the cook, for if the meals aren't good, the ship loses its crew.

14. If Miss Brown is not back from her holidays **by** Friday or does not bother to inform us when she will return, we will fire her. **69**

15. Your success **pleases** me very much! **72**

Übung 46

1. I was afraid when the plane had to land with only one engine, but the pilot made a perfect landing.

2. They all visited the meeting even though it was held in Miami, Florida, because their company had paid their expenses.

3. It enjoys us that you like teaching so much.

4. Was she here last week? Yes, we think.

5. I can't tell if this picture I'm hanging is crooked or not.

6. When the tax official informed the taxpayer that he owed five thousand dollars in back taxes, the man couldn't believe it. When he told him he must pay within a month, the taxpayer fainted.

7. He pounded in the nail with such energy that he cracked the wood of the table he was making.

8. Farmers have to work all days of the week.

9. How attractive you are to the opposite sex depends not only from your appearance; your personality also plays a role.

10. Since one can earn money right after finishing high school, many young people do not go on to get a higher education.

11. I am interested to see what the results of this turtle race will be.

12. I will do it then when I have time.

13. There gives no possibility that the money will be paid on time.

14. All what he did was to say that he disagreed, and his boss fired him.

15. Say me what your favorite meal is.

Lösung 46

1. I was afraid when the plane had to land with only one engine, but the pilot made a perfect landing.

2. They all **attended** the meeting even though it was held in Miami, Florida, because their company had paid their expenses. **78**

3. It **pleases** us that you like teaching so much. **72**

4. Was she here last week? Yes, we think **so.** **65**

5. I can't tell if this picture I'm hanging is crooked or not.

6. When the tax official informed the taxpayer that he owed five thousand dollars in back taxes, the man couldn't believe it. When he told him he **had to** pay within a month, the taxpayer fainted. **73**

7. He pounded in the nail with such energy that he cracked the wood of the table he was making.

8. Farmers have to work **every day** of the week. **79**

9. How attractive you are to the opposite sex depends not only **on** your appearance; your personality also plays a role. **77**

10. Since one can earn money right after finishing high school, many young people do not go on to get a higher education. **54**

11. I am interested **in seeing** what the results of this turtle race will be. **80**

12. I will do it **when** I have time. **81**

13. **There is** no possibility that the money will be paid on time. **82**

14. All **that** he did was to say that he disagreed, and his boss fired him. **71**

15. **Tell** me what your favorite meal is. **67**

Übung 47

1. There gives nothing you can say to comfort a person who has lost a loved one.
2. If all what you say about his being honest is true, why is he behind bars so often?
3. His boss told him to finish the project then when he returned.
4. He comes all three days but never stays very long.
5. His coming late surprised them all.
6. You sometimes hear people say that a man who doesn't have a profession until the age of thirty will never amount to anything in life.
7. If you stay telephoning all your friends each night, you'll drive us crazy. We want peace and quiet in the evening!
8. It needs a long time to restore a garden to its original good condition if it has been neglected awhile.
9. It is only a disaster to have a wife who can't cook if you can't, either.
10. Are you interested to increase your knowledge?
11. The funeral procession moved slowly down the main street blocking traffic as it went.
12. The children's answers enjoyed their grandfather, who chuckled for an hour afterward remembering them.
13. Do you want to buy ice cream now? Yesterday you said you wanted it.
14. My parents were in the theatre last night.
15. Because of a power failure, there was no electricity for 4 days.

Lösung 47

1. **There is** nothing you can say to comfort a person who has lost a loved one. **82**

2. If all **that** you say about his being honest is true, why is he behind bars so often? **71**

3. His boss told him to finish the project **when** he returned. **81**

4. He comes **every** three days but never stays very long. **79**

5. His coming late surprised them all. **74**

6. You sometimes hear people say that a man who doesn't have a profession **by** the age of thirty will never amount to anything in life. **69**

7. If you **keep** telephoning all your friends each night, you'll drive us crazy. We want peace and quiet in the evening! **75**

8. It **takes** a long time to restore a garden to its original good condition if it has been neglected awhile. **70**

9. It is only a disaster to have a wife who can't cook if you can't, either.

10. Are you interested **in increasing** your knowledge? **80**

11. The funeral procession moved slowly down the main street blocking traffic as it went.

12. The children's answers **pleased** their grandfather, who chuckled for an hour afterward remembering them. **72**

13. Do you want to buy ice cream now? Yesterday you said you wanted **to.** **65**

14. My parents were **at** the theatre last night. **83**

15. Because of a power failure, there was no electricity for 4 days.

Übung 48

1. You can't compare two things if the systems are another.
2. If a teacher says a pupil to be quiet and the pupil continues to disturb the class, the teacher has no choice but to throw him out.
3. I am interested to go swimming this weekend.
4. I know what for a great distance it is between the two cities.
5. It needed two days to clear the rubble from the tracks after the terrible train crash last month.
6. He is in charge of controlling the goods as they are brought into the store.
7. Thoreau disagreed with the notion that that what you say today must be maintained tomorrow. Such consistency, he claimed, was foolish.
8. They were surprised at his helping himself to a second piece of cake without asking first.
9. When he grew older he realized that good health was not something to be taken for granted.
10. The diplomats are required to visit all council meetings.
11. The boxer knew that he must get up before the referee counted to ten, but he had no fight left in him, so he lost.
12. Only three per cent of costs are due to an increase in personnel expenditure.
13. The woman called her husband in his office to find out if he had to work overtime.
14. The bell rings all two hours.
15. The divorcée depended from the monthly cheque from her ex-husband.

Lösung 48

1. You can't compare two things if the systems are **different.** **84**

2. If a teacher **tells** a pupil to be quiet and the pupil continues to disturb the class, the teacher has no choice but to throw him out. **67**

3. I am interested **in going** swimming this weekend. **80**

4. I know **what a** great distance it is between the two cities. **85**

5. It **took** two days to clear the rubble from the tracks after the terrible train crash last month. **70**

6. He is in charge of **checking** the goods as they are brought into the store. **76**

7. Thoreau disagreed with the notion that **what** you say today must be maintained tomorrow. Such consistency, he claimed, was foolish. **66**

8. They were surprised at his helping himself to a second piece of cake without asking first. **74**

9. When he grew older he realized that good health was not something to be taken for granted. **57**

10. The diplomats are required to **attend** all council meetings. **78**

11. The boxer knew that he **had to** get up before the referee counted to ten, but he had no fight left in him, so he lost. **73**

12. Only three per cent of costs **is** due to an increase in personnel expenditure. **68**

13. The woman called her husband **at** his office to find out if he had to work overtime. **83**

14. The bell rings **every** two hours. **79**

15. The divorcée depended **on** the monthly cheque from her ex-husband. **77**

Übung 49

1. She doesn't know what for a difficult task she has before her.

2. When the man said me that he had lost his money and needed the taxi fare to get home, I made the mistake of believing him.

3. We were angry when it began to rain during the picnic, but the rain lasted only a few minutes, and then we had beautiful weather again.

4. This pen isn't like the one I had before. The two pens are another.

5. I stayed working until I finished the job.

6. I tried to persuade my wife to go to see a film of Walt Disney.

7. The ticket agent controls each person's ticket as he passes through the gate.

8. That what some politicians say to get votes is amazing.

9. I'd rather have snow than rain, wouldn't you?

10. He told me if I wanted to visit him, I could ring him in his home between 5 and 6 p.m. every day.

11. Of the three hundred sheeps in the meadow, ten were killed by wolves.

12. Four per cent of voting-age people are in favour of the president's present policies.

13. When I went to school it was this way: when you made a spelling mistake you must write the word correctly fifty times.

14. Whispering, as well as talking, is hard on ones throat.

15. He bought her a diamond ring to celebrate their tenth wedding anniversary.

Lösung 49

1. She doesn't know **what a** difficult task she has before her. **85**

2. When the man **told** me that he had lost his money and needed the taxi fare to get home, I made the mistake of believing him. **67**

3. We were angry when it began to rain during the picnic, but the rain lasted only a few minutes, and then we had beautiful weather again.

4. This pen isn't like the one I had before. The two pens are **different. 84**

5. I **kept** working until I finished the job. **75**

6. I tried to persuade my wife to go to see a film **by** Walt Disney. **86**

7. The ticket agent **checks** each person's ticket as he passes through the gate. **76**

8. **What** some politicians say to get votes is amazing. **66**

9. I'd rather have snow than rain, wouldn't you?

10. He told me if I wanted to visit him, I could ring him **at** his home between 5 and 6 p.m. every day. **83**

11. Of the three hundred **sheep** in the meadow, ten were killed by wolves. **58**

12. Four per cent of voting-age people **is** in favour of the president's present policies. **68**

13. When I went to school it was this way: when you made a spelling mistake you **had to** write the word correctly fifty times. **73**

14. Whispering, as well as talking, is hard on ones throat.

15. He bought her a diamond ring to celebrate their tenth wedding anniversary.

Übung 50

1. I recognized him on his black tie.

2. He told me that he was interested to learn more about the matter.

3. He can visit her whenever he wants it.

4. She will marry in the next time.

5. Only her own mother knows what for a problem she has with spelling and reading.

6. Leaving the stove turned on when you leave home is dangerous.

7. "Stay working until I call you for supper," called his mother.

8. Only if you control each person will you find the thief. He dresses like any other employee.

9. The teacher was amazed at his daring to ask such a question.

10. It needed a long time for the teacher to convince the father that his son should not follow in his footsteps.

11. The two theories are not both equally useful in this case because they are another.

12. We don't have to have guests every weekend.

13. It gives many people who want to help you in life, but most of them want to help when you no longer need help.

14. The man said yes to the request because he was drunk. If he had been asked then when he was sober, he would have said no.

15. The man looked all over the house after his glasses which he had left on top of his head.

Lösung 50

1. I recognized him **by** his black tie. **86**

2. He told me that he was interested **in learning** more about the matter. **80**

3. He can visit her whenever he wants **to.** **65**

4. She will marry in the **near future.** **87**

5. Only her own mother knows **what a** problem she has with spelling and reading. **85**

6. Leaving the stove turned on when you leave home is dangerous.

7. "**Keep** working until I call you for supper," called his mother. **75**

8. Only if you **check** each person will you find the thief. He dresses like any other employee. **76**

9. The teacher was amazed at his daring to ask such a question. **74**

10. It **took** a long time for the teacher to convince the father that his son should not follow in his footsteps. **70**

11. The two theories are not both equally useful in this case because they are **different.** **84**

12. We don't have to have guests every weekend. **4**

13. **There are** many people who want to help you in life, but most of them want to help when you no longer need help. **82**

14. The man said yes to the request because he was drunk. If he had been asked **when** he was sober, he would have said no. **81**

15. The man looked all over the house **for** his glasses which he had left on top of his head. **88**

Übung 51

1. In the next time he'll be promoted.

2. They realize what for a long trip it will be.

3. They ate potatoes because potatoes enjoyed them.

4. Maybe the poor student doesn't really want to live with his parents, but beggars can't be choosers. He has to take it or leave it.

5. When the tyre was punctured it made "ppfffft."

6. The thighs are strong, and I have a good sense of balance, so I can ride horses quite well.

7. It's important to control the packages that people send by mail. Sometimes they contain dangerous items.

8. Since he didn't smoke, he didn't have cigarettes lying around the house.

9. I'm amazed that you managed to visit college for four years without learning a single foreign language.

10. On the radio, on television and in the newspapers, one is constantly confronted with the terrible fact that it gives millions of people who do not have enough to eat.

11. Because they are another we can't judge all three crimes the same way.

12. The both people realized that it would be more fun to live together.

13. You cannot break the blade of my knife easily because it is made from the finest steel.

14. The police caught the thief in the near of my house.

15. Rugs are not only pretty but useful. They keep a house warm.

Lösung 51

1. In the **near future** he'll be promoted. **87**

2. They realize **what a** long trip it will be. **85**

3. They ate potatoes because they **liked** potatoes. **72**

4. Maybe the poor student doesn't really want to live with his parents, but beggars can't be choosers. He has to take it or leave it.

5. When the tyre was punctured it **went** "ppfffft." **89**

6. **My** thighs are strong, and I have a good sense of balance, so I can ride horses quite well. **1**

7. It's important to **check** the packages that people send by mail. Sometimes they contain dangerous items. **76**

8. Since he didn't smoke, he didn't have cigarettes lying around the house. **54**

9. I'm amazed that you managed to **attend** college for four years without learning a single foreign language. **78**

10. On the radio, on television and in the newspapers, one is constantly confronted with the terrible fact that **there are** millions of people who do not have enough to eat. **82**

11. Because they are **different** we can't judge all three crimes the same way. **84**

12. **Both people** realized that it would be more fun to live together. **91**

13. You cannot break the blade of my knife easily because it is made **of** the finest steel. **90**

14. The police caught the thief **near** my house. **48**

15. Rugs are not only pretty but useful. They keep a house warm.

Übung 52

1. Happiness is something you will never find if you look after it.

2. When he was surprised, he made, "Wow!"

3. The opinion of the both men is that you cannot have success if you do not work.

4. I interest myself for good music.

5. When five percent of the people are unemployed, we can say that we are in a depression.

6. It is true that automobiles are made from steel, but the metal is so thin that the slightest accident is enough to cause damage that costs a lot of money.

7. His former fiancée is now his best friend's wife.

8. The young man quit his job. He felt working wasn't necessary.

9. She moves like a dancer and looks like a model.

10. A person who has had a serious operation knows what for a painful experience it is.

11. They buried their dead bird under a rose bush in the back yard.

12. That what you save today will be useful in the future.

13. They'll move into their new apartment in the next time.

14. Acting in a film is quite different from playing a part in a theatre presentation.

15. If you touch that hot pan, it'll burn you.

Lösung 52

1. Happiness is something you will never find if you look **for** it. **88**

2. When he was surprised, he **went,** "Wow!" **89**

3. The opinion of **both men** is that you cannot have success if you do not work. **91**

4. I **am interested in** good music. **92**

5. When five percent of the people **is** unemployed, we can say that we are in a depression. **68**

6. It is true that automobiles are made **of** steel, but the metal is so thin that the slightest accident is enough to cause damage that costs a lot of money. **90**

7. His former fiancée is now his best friend's wife.

8. The young man quit his job. He felt working wasn't necessary. **57**

9. She moves like a dancer and looks like a model.

10. A person who has had a serious operation knows **what a** painful experience it is. **85**

11. They buried their dead bird under a rose bush in the back yard.

12. **What** you save today will be useful in the future. **66**

13. They'll move into their new apartment in the **near future.** **87**

14. Acting in a film is quite different from playing a part in a theatre presentation.

15. If you touch that hot pan, it'll burn you.

Übung 53

1. For a person to overcome the loss of someone he loves needs time, but it is said that time heals all wounds.

2. All four weeks, the menu at the restaurant repeats itself.

3. He visited the class for five years without ever missing a day.

4. When he played the snare drums they made "rratt-ta-tat!"

5. A burglar can find valuables very easily without having to look after them very long, because almost all people hide such things in the same obvious places.

6. A person should not eat at pre-scheduled times, but then when he is hungry.

7. In the center of every major city in the world, it gives houses that should be torn down to make room for modern buildings.

8. The physician who interests himself for the total well-being of his patients is a rarity today.

9. The both men decided that they had worked long enough, and went out for a beer.

10. She will pay him a visit in the next time.

11. The only street that I have ever lived in for more than 10 years is the Woolman Court.

12. Because the Prime Minister was staying in the State Hotel for a few days, there was a constant crowd of reporters in the vicinity.

13. The book was written from Churchill.

14. You must go to the place to prove if you are right.

15. He said me that he wore straw shoes and a straw hat in summer.

Lösung 53

1. For a person to overcome the loss of someone he loves **takes** time, but it is said that time heals all wounds. **70**

2. **Every** four weeks, the menu at the restaurant repeats itself. **79**

3. He **attended** the class for five years without ever missing a day. **78**

4. When he played the snare drums they **went** "ratt-ta-tat!" **89**

5. A burglar can find valuables very easily without having to look **for** them very long, because almost all people hide such things in the same obvious places. **88**

6. A person should not eat at pre-scheduled times, but **when** he is hungry. **81**

7. In the center of every major city in the world, **there are** houses that should be torn down to make room for modern buildings. **82**

8. The physician who **is interested in** the total well-being of his patients is a rarity today. **92**

9. **Both men** decided that they had worked long enough, and went out for a beer. **91**

10. She will pay him a visit in the **near future.** **87**

11. The only street that I have ever lived in for more than 10 years is **Woolman Court.** **5**

12. Because the Prime Minister was staying **at** the State Hotel for a few days, there was a constant crowd of reporters in the vicinity. **83**

13. The book was written **by** Churchill. **86**

14. You must go to the place to **check** if you are right. **93**

15. He **told** me that he wore straw shoes and a straw hat in summer. **67**

Übung 54

1. When we say this in German we mean something other.

2. When you said we should plan to depart from Rome instead of Milan you took the words right out of my mouth!

3. Nowadays, automobiles are equipped with ventilators that replace the air in the passenger compartment all three minutes.

4. He interests himself for diving, even though he can't swim a stroke.

5. Get busy and clean up your room! It's horribly messy.

6. If the young girl had returned home then when she promised her parents she would, they would not have worried.

7. Everyone who has an own car is required to pay taxes on it.

8. If he listened, we would not have to say everything twice.

9. The carp they ate for dinner had been swimming in a tank three hours before.

10. The man who looks before he leaps will have fewer disasters than the man who never plans ahead.

11. In the first time we ate a lot of butter, but after we learned that it was not healthy to do so, we ate less.

12. Underneath the oil painting, the experts found another that was said to be from Rembrandt.

13. I'm pretty smart, but my sister's still smarter.

14. The bank manager said he'd prove the account personally, since there seemed to be so much trouble about deciding how much money had been overdrawn.

15. No insurance company wanted to insure the house made from wood.

Lösung 54

1. When we say this in German we mean something **else.** **94**

2. When you said we should plan to depart from Rome instead of Milan you took the words right out of my mouth!

3. Nowadays automobiles are equipped with ventilators that replace the air in the passenger compartment **every** three minutes. **79**

4. He **is interested in** diving, even though he can't swim a stroke. **92**

5. Get busy and clean up your room! It's horribly messy.

6. If the young girl had returned home **when** she promised her parents she would, they would not have worried. **81**

7. Everyone who has **his** own car is required to pay taxes on it. **95**

8. If he listened, we would not have to say everything twice.

9. The carp they ate for dinner had been swimming in a tank three hours before.

10. The man who looks before he leaps will have fewer disasters than the man who never plans ahead.

11. **At first** we ate a lot of butter, but after we learned that it was not healthy to do so, we ate less. **7**

12. Underneath the oil painting, the experts found another that was said to be **by** Rembrandt. **86**

13. I'm pretty smart, but my sister's **even** smarter. **51**

14. The bank manager said he'd **check** the account personally, since there seemed to be so much trouble about deciding how much money had been overdrawn. **93**

15. No insurance company wanted to insure the house made **of** wood. **90**

Übung 55

1. Return this and buy something other that is less expensive.

2. He took the both children with him.

3. It's my meaning that she only bats her eyelashes because she thinks it looks cute.

4. If they had seen the girl that sold them the broken watch last week they would have complained to her.

5. I'll prove his story to see if it's true.

6. If you do everything you have to do then when you should do it, things will never pile up and become unmanageable.

7. If you are interested to buy the house then you have to act quickly because there are many others who are also interested.

8. Japan has no own raw materials and must therefore depend upon other countries for them.

9. What did wake the man up?

10. The girl had no personality of her own. Everything she did depended from the wishes of her fiancé.

11. To interest yourself for the finer things of life is not a question of wealth or social standing, but one of intelligence, sensitivity, and the ability to discriminate.

12. Their favorite cousin lived in Puerto Rico for three years.

13. Sometimes it is more fun to look after something than to find it.

14. The dog made "Gggrrrr!" whenever it saw a stranger.

15. I've heard that somewhere on earth a person dies of cancer all thirty seconds.

Lösung 55

1. Return this and buy something **else** that is less expensive. **94**
2. He took the **two** children with him. **91**
3. It's my **opinion** that she only bats her eyelashes because she thinks it looks cute. **15**
4. If they had seen the girl that sold them the broken watch last week, they would have complained to her. **17**
5. I'll **check** his story to see if it's true. **93**
6. If you do everything you have to do **when** you should do it, things will never pile up and become unmanageable. **81**
7. If you are interested **in buying** the house then you have to act quickly because there are many others who are also interested. **80**
8. Japan has no raw materials **of its own** and must therefore depend upon other countries for them. **95**
9. What **woke** the man up? **2**
10. The girl had no personality of her own. Everything she did depended **on** the wishes of her fiancé. **77**
11. To **be interested in** the finer things of life is not a question of wealth or social standing, but one of intelligence, sensitivity, and the ability to discriminate. **92**
12. Their favorite cousin lived in Puerto Rico for three years.
13. Sometimes it is more fun to look **for** something than to find it. **88**
14. The dog **went** "Gggrrrr!" whenever it saw a stranger. **89**
15. I've heard that somewhere on earth a person dies of cancer **every** thirty seconds. **79**

Übung 56

1. Don't give me fish every night! Give me something other once in a while!

2. How interested you are to learn something depends on how motivated you are.

3. Whether a country wins or loses a war seldom depends from the morale of the soldiers.

4. The police proved the suspect's alibi.

5. He interests himself for those countries that don't interest other people. That's why he has such quiet vacations.

6. When a cat goes fishing it is faced with a crisis: it likes fish, but it hates getting wet!

7. A great thinker once remarked that a man without an own opinion is the poorest of creatures.

8. Thirty-five per cent of all marriages of people under twenty are destined to fail.

9. Are they still waiting for us? I'd have thought they'd have gone by now!

10. The both girls who won the beauty contest got bouquets of red roses.

11. After the English lesson the pupils do go out for a beer.

12. The windows of the President's limousine were made from bullet-proof glass.

13. Her sister is married with an army officer.

14. Our train will arrive London at 2 p.m.

15. The snake made "Ssssst!" when it was disturbed.

Lösung 56

1. Don't give me fish every night! Give me something **else** once in a while! **94**

2. How interested you are **in learning** something depends on how motivated you are. **80**

3. Whether a country wins or loses a war seldom depends **on** the morale of the soldiers. **77**

4. The police **checked** the suspect's alibi. **93**

5. He **is interested in** those countries that don't interest other people. That's why he has such quiet vacations. **92**

6. When a cat goes fishing it is faced with a crisis: it likes fish, but it hates getting wet!

7. A great thinker once remarked that a man without **his** own opinion is the poorest of creatures. **95**

8. Thirty-five per cent of all marriages of people under twenty **is** destined to fail. **68**

9. Are they still waiting for us? I'd have thought they'd have gone by now!

10. **Both** girls who won the beauty contest got bouquets of red roses. **91**

11. After the English lesson the pupils **go** out for a beer. **96**

12. The windows of the President's limousine were made **of** bullet-proof glass. **90**

13. Her sister is married **to** an army officer. **97**

14. Our train will arrive **in** London at 2 p.m. **98**

15. The snake **went** "Sssssst" when it was disturbed. **89**

Übung 57

1. Until a housewife gains experience, she always does burn the meals.

2. The brothers look alike, but their personalities are another.

3. If your worrying about the sick cat is keeping you awake, take it to the vet.

4. People say that he has connections with gangsters.

5. When something is difficult to find we say, "It is like looking after a needle in a haystack."

6. Without an own car you are dependent on public means of transportation.

7. A little self-discipline is all one needs to be on time.

8. To be happy, everyone needs to feel he has a specialty or a talent.

9. If there gives anything that I cannot stand, it is someone who slurps his soup.

10. Which language speak you, Chinese or Arabic?

11. I have made a note of his birthday on my calendar, so it is not necessary for you to remember me of this date again.

12. Did you visit the National Convention when it met in New York last week for its annual meeting of shareholders?

13. The woman told the shop girl that she wanted to buy a blouse made from the finest silk.

14. We regret to have to inform you that our plane will arrive Chicago one hour late.

15. They wrote that we would be getting a package in the next time.

Lösung 57

1. Until a housewife gains experience, she always **burns** the meals. **96**

2. The brothers look alike, but their personalities are **different.** **84**

3. If your worrying about the sick cat is keeping you awake, take it to the vet. **74**

4. People say that he has connections **to** gangsters. **97**

5. When something is difficult to find we say, "It is like looking **for** a needle in a haystack." **88**

6. Without **your** own car you are dependent on public means of transportation. **95**

7. A little self-discipline is all one needs to be on time. **62**

8. To be happy, everyone needs to feel he has a specialty or a talent.

9. If **there is** anything that I cannot stand, it is someone who slurps his soup. **82**

10. Which language **do you speak?** Chinese or Arabic? **2**

11. I have made a note of his birthday on my calendar, so it is not necessary for you to **remind** me of this date again. **99**

12. Did you **attend** the National Convention when it met in New York last week for its annual meeting of shareholders? **78**

13. The woman told the shop girl that she wanted to buy a blouse made **of** the finest silk. **90**

14. We regret to have to inform you that our plane will arrive **in** Chicago one hour late. **98**

15. They wrote that we would be getting a package in the **near future.** **87**

Übung 58

1. Any house owner can tell you that although an own house is a wonderful thing, it is never so cheap as a rented one.

2. I decided to stay in my parents' home the whole weekend.

3. This remembers me of my mother.

4. In his position as foreman he has the authority to give orders.

5. He decided to paint the baby's room with a special paint that could be written on. He must spend all afternoon working on it.

6. I hate travelling with a lot of luggage. I always lose something.

7. With the help of the tugboats the steamer was able to depart Cherbourg with a delay of only one hour.

8. It's more effective to reward someone for doing something well than to punish him for doing something wrong.

9. If you want to be able to deal with men of all nationalities, you should speak other languages beside English.

10. While he was talking, a butterfly flew into the room.

11. The both cities were very similar in size, but they were different in character.

12. Whether you come in April or May is equal to us. Either time is good for us.

13. You haven't finished. Stay working until you get it done.

14. Because the student interested himself for so many subjects, he couldn't decide what he wanted to make his life's work.

15. He usually gets handkerchiefs for Christmas. He wants to get something other this year.

Lösung 58

1. Any house owner can tell you that although **your own** house is a wonderful thing, it is never so cheap as a rented one. **95**

2. I decided to stay **at** my parents' home the whole weekend. **83**

3. This **reminds** me of my mother. **99**

4. In his position **of** foreman he has the authority to give orders. **100**

5. He decided to paint the baby's room with a special paint that could be written on. He **had to** spend all afternoon working on it. **73**

6. I hate travelling with a lot of luggage. I always lose something.

7. With the help of the tugboats the steamer was able to depart **from** Cherbourg with a delay of only one hour. **98**

8. It's more effective to reward someone for doing something well than to punish him for doing something wrong.

9. If you want to be able to deal with men of all nationalities, you should speak other languages **besides** English. **101**

10. While he was talking, a butterfly flew into the room.

11. The **two** cities were very similar in size, but they were different in character. **91**

12. Whether you come in April or May **doesn't matter** to us. Either time is good for us. **19**

13. You haven't finished. **Keep** working until you get it done. **75**

14. Because the student **was interested in** so many subjects, he couldn't decide what he wanted to make his life's work. **92**

15. He usually gets handkerchiefs for Christmas. He wants to get something **else** this year. **94**

Übung 59

1. To be a good wife you have to be able to do something beside cook.

2. See over here! I have found your lost pin under the couch.

3. A secretary is an indispensable person. The things she remembers you of that you would otherwise forget make her worth her weight in gold.

4. I can't eat rice with chopsticks. I need a fork.

5. I've been waiting for a letter from you since ages.

6. I'm really lucky. You came in the nick of time.

7. Who has an empty head talks loudest.

8. Gangsters pay certain sums of money to the police to be permitted to park there where parking is prohibited.

9. He orders all the new machines for his department in his position as shop manager.

10. The young man is attached with his dog. They do everything together.

11. The car's headlights shined on the wet street.

12. A man, no matter how experienced, can never begin a business with no own capital.

13. The children decided to present a play, but they spent so much time arguing about who would have the title role that they never gave the play.

14. Talk to someone other about that problem. I can't help you.

15. I was used to have my own way when I was little.

Lösung 59

1. To be a good wife you have to be able to do something **besides** cook. **101**

2. **Look** over here! I have found your lost pin under the couch. **11**

3. A secretary is an indispensable person. The things she **reminds** you of that you would otherwise forget make her worth her weight in gold. **99**

4. I can't eat rice with chopsticks. I need a fork.

5. I've been waiting for a letter from you **for** ages. **3**

6. I'm really lucky. You came in the nick of time.

7. **Whoever** has an empty head talks loudest. **6**

8. Gangsters pay certain sums of money to the police to be permitted to park **where** parking is prohibited. **102**

9. He orders all the new machines for his department in his position **of** shop manager. **100**

10. The young man is attached **to** his dog. They do everything together. 97

11. The car's headlight **shone** on the wet street. **27**

12. A man, no matter how experienced, can never begin a business with no capital **of his own.** **95**

13. The children decided to present a play, but they spent so much time arguing about who would have the title role that they never gave the play.

14. Talk to someone **else** about that problem. I can't help you. **94**

15. I was used to **having** my own way when I was little. **38**

Übung 60

1. That organ music is by Bach. I know the piece well, because I'm interested to study baroque organ music.

2. Whether or not I give you permission to go depends from your behavior during the next week.

3. Her little sister was more independent than she was, and didn't like to hold anyone's hand when she crossed streets.

4. As a punishment for having lied, Billy had to stay in school an extra hour.

5. The young couple saved a lot of money by having its furniture made from an old carpenter whose work was good but inexpensive.

6. The man who had said something insulting looked after a way out.

7. Those two buses are another. Be careful which one you take.

8. I realize what for a hard job it is to write a book.

9. When he returned to his place of birth it remembered him of his youth.

10. If the plane arrives Hamburg within the next ten minutes, the passengers will be able to catch the connecting flight to London.

11. They will have been married to each other for thirty years in July.

12. The boy wanted to play the drums, but he had to play the piano instead.

13. You have to send the letter to him there where he lives, because we don't know his business address.

14. In his capacity as concert master he has to tune up the orchestra before concerts.

15. We listen with the teacher when the teacher speaks.

Lösung 60

1. That organ music is by Bach. I know the piece well, because I'm interested **in studying** baroque organ music. **80**

2. Whether or not I give you permission to go depends **on** your behavior during the next week. **77**

3. Her little sister was more independent than she was, and didn't like to hold anyone's hand when she crossed streets.

4. As a punishment for having lied, Billy had to stay **at** school an extra hour. **83**

5. The young couple saved a lot of money by having its furniture made **by** an old carpenter whose work was good but inexpensive. **86**

6. The man who had said something insulting looked **for** a way out. **88**

7. Those two buses are **different.** Be careful which one you take. **84**

8. I realize **what a** hard job it is to write a book. **85**

9. When he returned to his place of birth it **reminded** him of his youth. **99**

10. If the plane arrives **in** Hamburg within the next ten minutes, the passengers will be able to catch the connecting flight to London. **98**

11. They will have been married to each other for thirty years in July.

12. The boy wanted to play the drums, but he had to play the piano instead.

13. You have to send the letter to him **where** he lives, because we don't know his business address. **102**

14. In his capacity **of** concert master he has to tune up the orchestra before concerts. **100**

15. We listen **to** the teacher when the teacher speaks. **97**

Übung 61

1. During the last years I have not had the success I feel I should have had.

2. I wish I were rich. Then I would visit the horse races, and bet on a horse.

3. Never get married with a divorced man.

4. Her job is controlling the visitors.

5. When you are late you must excuse yourself.

6. We heard the speaker carefully as he outlined his objections to the government.

7. If he hadn't made his job well, he would have been fired.

8. In the next time he hopes to get a pet monkey.

9. When he called them up, the telephone made "Brrring!"

10. He usually treats his wife good.

11. There's a lot of water in the Elbe, but in the brook near our summer cottage there's only a little.

12. When I looked at my watch I saw that I would be 10 minutes too late.

13. He doesn't like his fiancée. He wants to marry someone other.

14. During going down the street I met an old friend.

15. Look after my turtle for me while I'm gone, and be sure to feed it on time.

Lösung 61

1. During **the last few years** I have not had the success I feel I should have had. **103**

2. I wish I were rich. Then I would **attend** the horse races, and bet on a horse. **78**

3. Never get married **to** a divorced man. **97**

4. Her job is **checking** the visitors. **76**

5. When you are late you must **apologize.** **104**

6. We **listened to** the speaker carefully as he outlined his objections to the government. **10**

7. If he hadn't **done** his job well, he would have been fired. **8**

8. In the **near future** he hopes to get a pet monkey. **87**

9. When he called them up, the telephone **went** "Brrring!" **89**

10. He usually treats his wife **well.** **9**

11. There's a lot of water in the Elbe, but in the brook near our summer cottage there's only a little.

12. When I looked at my watch I saw that I would be 10 minutes **late.** **33**

13. He doesn't like his financée. He wants to marry someone **else.** **94**

14. **While** going down the street I met an old friend. **105**

15. Look after my turtle for me while I'm gone, and be sure to feed it on time. **62**

Übung 62

1. I must excuse myself for interrupting you.

2. He isn't usually playing football during the week.

3. In his position as boss, that man approves or rejects the proposals presented by his employees.

4. He had already left the house when she called.

5. If you have no toothpaste, salt and soda are a good substitute.

6. It gives people who never write letters.

7. The cookies were so old they were stale, so we had to feed them to the ducks in the park.

8. Are they here already? I thought they wouldn't have arrived yet!

9. They tried to cross the street there where there was no crosswalk and were nearly run over by a car.

10. It's hard to learn to share things with others, especially then when you are young.

11. Children can be cruel.

12. When do you smoke, when you're tense, or when you're bored? I find I smoke all five minutes when I'm bored.

13. She saw Santa Claus during entering the department store's toy department.

14. It took him two years to recover from the car accident.

15. The teacher sat up all night proving the pupils' homework.

Lösung 62

1. I must **apologize** for interrupting you. **104**

2. He **doesn't** usually **play** football during the week. **12**

3. In his position **of** boss, that man approves or rejects the proposals presented by his employees. **100**

4. He had already left the house when she called.

5. If you have no toothpaste, salt and soda are a good substitute.

6. **There are** people who never write letters. **82**

7. The cookies were so old they were stale, so we had to feed them to the ducks in the park.

8. Are they here already? I thought they wouldn't have arrived yet!

9. They tried to cross the street **where there** was no crosswalk and were nearly run over by a car. **102**

10. It's hard to learn to share things with others, especially **when** you are young. **81**

11. Children can be cruel.

12. When do you smoke, when you're tense, or when you're bored? I find I smoke **every** five minutes when I'm bored. **79**

13. She saw Santa Claus **while** entering the department store's toy department. **105**

14. It took him two years to recover from the car accident.

15. The teacher sat up all night **checking** the pupils' homework. **93**

Übung 63

1. He has seen so many animals at the zoo last Saturday that he can't remember what an antelope looks like. He confuses it with the armadillo.

2. He wasn't afraid of making mistakes in a foreign language.

3. If you do lie down for a while at noon you will find that you will be able to accomplish more in the afternoon.

4. A football coach must be able to overlook the whole and plan his strategy accordingly.

5. I am flying from Hamburg to New York and will change the plane in Frankfurt.

6. There isn't someone on the phone.

7. I don't know why you didn't tell us years ago that you'd been divorced. I didn't know it, and my wife didn't know it, too.

8. Children shouldn't be rude with their elders.

9. The modern jet airliners are flown from pilots who have been carefully trained.

10. In his position as office manager he can make changes in the arrangement of office furniture in his department.

11. After the storm, there was a rainbow.

12. How do you call your cat, Lily or Silly?

13. We'll prove if he came on last night's train. Perhaps he didn't.

14. If I had the money, I'd go to Florida for Christmas.

15. I like you and consider you to be my friend because we interest ourselves for the same things.

Lösung 63

1. He **saw** so many animals at the zoo last Saturday that he can't remember what an antelope looks like. He confuses it with the armadillo. **13**

2. He wasn't afraid of making mistakes in a foreign language.

3. If you **lie** down for a while at noon you will find that you will be able to accomplish more in the afternoon. **96**

4. A football coach must be able to **oversee** the whole and plan his strategy accordingly. **35**

5. I am flying from Hamburg to New York and will change **planes** in Frankfurt. **106**

6. There isn't **anyone** on the phone. **14**

7. I don't know why you didn't tell us years ago that you'd been divorced. I didn't know it, and my wife didn't know it, **either.** **16**

8. Children shouldn't be rude **to** their elders. **97**

9. The modern jet airliners are flown **by** pilots who have been carefully trained. **86**

10. In his position **of** office manager he can make changes in the arrangement of office furniture in his department. **100**

11. After the storm, there was a rainbow.

12. **What** do you call your cat, Lily or Silly? **28**

13. We'll **check** if he came on last night's train. Perhaps he didn't. **93**

14. If I had the money, I'd go to Florida for Christmas.

15. I like you and consider you to be my friend because we **are interested in** the same things. **92**

Übung 64

1. When you take language lessons it is not good to change the teacher too often.

2. She cleaned the furnitures until they shone, and then she scrubbed the floor.

3. Her new shoes squeaked when she walked.

4. Beside eating fruit you must eat vegetables to get all the vitamins you need.

5. They had planned to go to an organ concert that evening, but had to give up the idea because they were so tired.

6. Leave the dog outside. Tie it there where you tied it the last time.

7. There is nothing more frustrating than living in a city that has a fine opera, and not having enough money to go.

8. The three armed bandits wore black masks and black jackets. They met in the corner of the street.

9. Skinning chickens makes me sick. I let my husband do it.

10. It's not only a beautiful necklace, but also a valuable one. My grandmother gave it to me for forty years.

11. He has been earning a large salary during the past years.

12. If you do sit at a desk all day and never get any exercise, your heart will suffer in the long run.

13. We excuse ourselves for not having come sooner.

14. Whenever I was lazy, my mother would remind me, "The devil finds work for idle hands to do." I hated that advice like the plague.

15. What good does it do to talk to you, if you never listen?

Lösung 64

1. When you take language lessons it is not good to change **teachers** too often. **106**

2. She cleaned the **furniture** until **it** shone, and then she scrubbed the floor. **58**

3. Her new shoes squeaked when she walked.

4. **Besides** eating fruit you must eat vegetables to get all the vitamins you need. **101**

5. They had planned to go to an organ concert that evening, but had to give up the idea because they were so tired.

6. Leave the dog outside. Tie it **where** you tied it the last time. **102**

7. There is nothing more frustrating than living in a city that has a fine opera, and not having enough money to go.

8. The three armed bandits wore black masks and black jackets. They met **at** the corner of the street. **83**

9. Skinning chickens makes me sick. I let my husband do it.

10. It's not only a beautiful necklace, but also a valuable one. My grandmother gave it to me **forty years ago.** **18**

11. He has been earning a large salary during **the past few years.** **103**

12. If you **sit** at a desk all day and never get any exercise, your heart will suffer in the long run. **96**

13. We **apologize** for not having come sooner. **104**

14. Whenever I was lazy, my mother would remind me, "The devil finds work for idle hands to do." I hated that advice like the plague.

15. What good does it do to talk to you, if you never listen?

Übung 65

1. He came home late so he missed seeing the visitors.
2. He is the type of individual who does greet anyone, even if the person is a total stranger.
3. Someone beside me better be there! I refuse to face the teacher alone!
4. He insisted to keep his old pants, even after they had got holes at the knees.
5. She gave sometimes her friend flowers.
6. More than four months passed since I came here.
7. You have so few tea in your cup it's hardly worth drinking. Let me pour you some more.
8. If you shout at her and I one more time, we'll quit!
9. A parrot whose master is Turkish will never speak Greek.
10. War memorials should remember us of the terrible price the world has had to pay for ending disputes with force.
11. She said she had to excuse herself because she hadn't written any letters to her friend for two months.
12. Bring this book upstairs to your mother.
13. The lady asked the pet shop owner what for a white dog they had.
14. They departed Miami earlier than they had expected.
15. He is yet here.

Lösung 65

1. He came home late so he missed seeing the visitors.

2. He is the type of individual who **greets** anyone, even if the person is a total stranger. **96**

3. Someone **besides** me better be there! I refuse to face the teacher alone! **101**

4. He insisted **on keeping** his old pants, even after they had got holes at the knees. **107**

5. She **sometimes gave** her friend flowers. **20**

6. More than four months **have passed** since I came here. **108**

7. You have so **little** tea in your cup it's hardly worth drinking. Let me pour you some more. **21**

8. If you shout at her and **me** one more time, we'll quit! **22**

9. A parrot whose master is Turkish will never speak Greek. **41**

10. War memorials should **remind** us of the terrible price the world has had to pay for ending disputes with force. **99**

11. She said she had to **apologize** because she hadn't written any letters to her friend for two months. **104**

12. **Take** this book upstairs to your mother. **32**

13. The lady asked the pet shop owner **what kind of a** white dog they had. **85**

14. They departed **from** Miami earlier than they had expected. **98**

15. He is **still** here. **109**

Übung 66

1. The secretary insisted to leave the office at exactly 5 p.m. every day.

2. In his position as major general he has many men's obedience.

3. She used to take a flashlight to bed with her so she could read after her mother had turned off the lights.

4. Eat the meal in the kitchen there where you should, not in here where you'll spill it on the rug.

5. He is not here already.

6. I have eaten wonderful meals at that restaurant. I ate there only last month, and enjoyed myself enormously.

7. If a man is yet unmarried and thirty-nine years old then we call him a confirmed bachelor.

8. Since she left the firm, we had nothing but trouble!

9. The lady ran to catch the bus, but because she had her two small children with her, she didn't get to the bus in time to take it.

10. He hasn't done anything wrong yet, but I expect him to at any moment.

11. She played the piano beside playing the flute.

12. A glance at the clock remembered the businessman that if he didn't complete his work soon he would miss his plane.

13. During the last years we haven't seen each other often.

14. They excused themselves for causing trouble.

15. The boy was a loner and liked to play by himself.

Lösung 66

1. The secretary insisted **on leaving** the office at exactly 5 p.m. every day. **107**

2. In his position **of** major general he has many men's obedience. **100**

3. She used to take a flashlight to bed with her so she could read after her mother had turned off the lights.

4. Eat the meal in the kitchen **where** you should, not in here where you'll spill it on the rug. **102**

5. He is not here **yet.** **110**

6. I have eaten wonderful meals at that restaurant. I ate there only last month, and enjoyed myself enormously.

7. If a man is **still** unmarried and thirty-nine years old then we call him a confirmed bachelor. **109**

8. Since she left the firm, we **have had** nothing but trouble! **108**

9. The lady ran to catch the bus, but because she had her two small children with her, she didn't get to the bus in time to take it.

10. He hasn't done anything wrong yet, but I expect him to at any moment.

11. She played the piano **besides** playing the flute. **101**

12. A glance at the clock **reminded** the businessman that if he didn't complete his work soon he would miss his plane. **99**

13. During **the last few years** we haven't seen each other often. **103**

14. They **apologized** for causing trouble. **104**

15. The boy was a loner and liked to play by himself.

Übung 67

1. The plane cannot start already because the food for the flight has not been brought on board.

2. The both dogs are black poodles.

3. He sang arias when he took a shower, and drove the rest of his family crazy.

4. He discovered that the girl getting married that day was an own daughter.

5. If you insist to hear the whole story then you had better sit down for it is a long one.

6. Because their dog had fourteen puppies instead of the expected six, they had a terrible time finding homes for all the little dogs.

7. He put the chair back there where it belonged.

8. They exclaimed about what for a beautiful street it was.

9. Since we came to Germany we didn't see a real skyscraper.

10. The tall, thin young lady with a long nose liked to eat whole cucumbers.

11. If you have eaten a three course meal and are yet hungry, you should consult a doctor. You have to learn more about your rate of metabolism and how to adjust to it.

12. She must excuse herself for having been careless.

13. When he died, his son had to overtake the family business.

14. Will you help me look after my lost dog?

15. You can't solve this problem like the one you had before because it is another.

Lösung 67

1. The plane cannot start **yet** because the food for the flight has not been brought on board. **110**

2. **Both** dogs are black poodles. **91**

3. He sang arias when he took a shower, and drove the rest of his family crazy.

4. He discovered that the girl getting married that day was **his own** daughter. **95**

5. If you insist **on hearing** the whole story then you had better sit down for it is a long one. **107**

6. Because their dog had fourteen puppies instead of the expected six, they had a terrible time finding homes for all the little dogs.

7. He put the chair back **where** it belonged. **102**

8. They exclaimed about **what a** beautiful street it was. **85**

9. Since we came to Germany we **haven't seen** a real skyscraper. **108**

10. The tall, thin young lady with a long nose liked to eat whole cucumbers.

11. If you have eaten a three course meal and are **still** hungry, you should consult a doctor. You have to learn more about your rate of metabolism and how to adjust to it. **109**

12. She must **apologize** for having been careless. **104**

13. When he died, his son had to **take over** the family business. **111**

14. Will you help me look **for** my lost dog? **88**

15. You can't solve this problem like the one you had before because it is **different.** **84**

Übung 68

1. During skating he fell down and broke his leg. As a consequence he could not earn the money he was accustomed to.

2. The ladies did their own sewing and made dresses for them because they didn't want to have to pay a tailor.

3. It was a year since I saw him.

4. We stood in class an extra hour to make up for a lesson we had missed.

5. He said he wished he were a bird so he could fly.

6. To look attractive you don't have to do anything beside smile.

7. She likes boots that come up to her knees better than short boots, but the longer the boots, the more they cost.

8. The customer asked what for a portable radio under thirty dollars the store had.

9. A travelling salesman who changes the town very often begins to feel at home in every town after a while.

10. Although the patient was very ill, he insisted to walk without the aid of crutches.

11. I'll overtake this job of yours if you have too many duties.

12. In his position as vice-president he must take over the president's tasks when the latter is ill.

13. It was a two hours long eclipse.

14. In no other country have I seen so many well-dressed women.

15. At first the housewife went shopping, then she cooked, and then she rested.

Lösung 68

1. **While** skating he fell down and broke his leg. As a consequence he could not earn the money was accustomed to. **105**

2. The ladies did their own sewing and made dresses for **themselves** because they didn't want to have to pay a tailor. **23**

3. It **has been** a year since I saw him. **108**

4. We **stayed** in class an extra hour to make up for a lesson we had missed. **40**

5. He said he wished he were a bird so he could fly.

6. To look attractive you don't have to do anything **besides** smile. **101**

7. She likes boots that come up to her knees better than short boots, but the longer the boots, the more they cost.

8. The customer asked **what kind of a** portable radio under thirty dollars the store had. **85**

9. A travelling salesman who changes **towns** very often begins to feel at home in every town after a while. **106**

10. Although the patient was very ill, he insisted **on walking** without the aid of crutches. **107**

11. I'll **take over** this job of yours if you have too many duties. **111**

12. In his position **of** vice-president he must take over the president's tasks when the latter is ill. **100**

13. It was a two **hour** long eclipse. **24**

14. In no other country have I seen so many well-dressed women. **44**

15. **First** the housewife went shopping, then she cooked, and then she rested. **112**

Übung 69

1. They've been repairing the old farmhouse during the last years.

2. At first she gave him his coat, and then she kissed him goodbye.

3. While his wife was working, the man overtook the housework.

4. In his capacity as tax consultant he visits many different firms.

5. He doesn't pay any attention to his elder son, but he spoils the baby.

6. Researchers have found that it is very difficult to get cigarette smokers to change the brand.

7. During going on a routine patrol, the soldiers unexpectedly encountered a whole regiment of enemy troops.

8. If all what you needed was money, why didn't you ask me for a loan?

9. If you have slept ten hours and are yet tired when you get up, perhaps it means that it's time you went on vacation.

10. At noon, the Persian cat lay in the grass and tried to cool off, because it was so hot.

11. The child, wrapped in a bath towel, came into the living room to say goodnight to his father.

12. They wanted to choose their gifts themselves.

13. Will they become a refrigerator when it is summer?

14. What is interesting on this sentence is not the syntax.

15. I excuse myself for making so much noise.

Lösung 69

1. They've been repairing the old farmhouse during **the last few years.** **103**

2. **First** she gave him his coat, and then she kissed him goodbye. **112**

3. While his wife was working, the man **took over** the housework. **111**

4. In his capacity **of** tax consultant he visits many different firms. **100**

5. He doesn't pay any attention to his elder son, but he spoils the baby.

6. Researchers have found that it is very difficult to get cigarette smokers to change **brands.** **106**

7. **While** going on a routine patrol, the soldiers unexpectedly encountered a whole regiment of enemy troops. **105**

8. If all **that** you needed was money, why didn't you ask me for a loan? **71**

9. If you have slept ten hours and are **still** tired when you get up, perhaps it means that it's time you went on vacation. **109**

10. At noon, the Persian cat lay in the grass and tried to cool off, because it was so hot. **47**

11. The child, wrapped in a bath towel, came into the living room to say goodnight to his father.

12. They wanted to choose their gifts themselves.

13. Will they **get** a refrigerator when it is summer? **42**

14. What is interesting **about** this sentence is not the syntax. **113**

15. I **apologize** for making so much noise. **104**

Übung 70

1. Beside working all day, she also has a vegetable garden and three small children to care for.

2. If you insist to go out without an overcoat in such cold weather, at least put on a warm pullover.

3. At first the secretary cleaned the typewriter and then she typed.

4. It looks suspicious if you arrive a hotel without any luggage.

5. We wrote the firm a letter requesting some information, but have not received a reply already.

6. I have not seen him for long years.

7. There's nothing interesting on their wedding. I've seen dozens of weddings like it.

8. Heavy drinking, what is an increasing problem in modern society, is expensive and bad for ones health.

9. The man changed the table at the restaurant because no waiter seemed to be serving his table.

10. The new man will replace the school principal, overtaking all his duties.

11. At six in the morning the cock made "Cock-a-doodle-doo!"

12. The old man ever chews tobacco, and spits on the floor.

13. If you have a lot of money and are still not happy then take my advice: make more money!

14. A girl who does go dancing every night must be popular.

15. I am considered as a model of virtue.

Lösung 70

1. **Besides** working all day, she also has a vegetable garden and three small children to care for. **101**

2. If you insist **on going** out without an overcoat in such cold weather, at least put on a warm pullover. **107**

3. **First** the secretary cleaned the typewriter and then she typed. **112**

4. It looks suspicious if you arrive **at** a hotel without any luggage. **98**

5. We wrote the firm a letter requesting some information, but have not received a reply **yet.** **110**

6. I have not seen him for **many** years. **114**

7. There's nothing interesting **about** their wedding. I've seen dozens of weddings like it. **113**

8. Heavy drinking, **which** is an increasing problem in modern society, is expensive and bad for one's health. **25**

9. The man changed **tables** at the restaurant because no waiter seemed to be serving his table. **106**

10. The new man will replace the school principal, **taking over** all his duties. **111**

11. At six in the morning the cock **went** "Cock-a-doodle-doo!" **89**

12. The old man **always** chews tobacco, and spits on the floor. **26**

13. If you have a lot of money and are **yet** not happy then take my advice: make more money! **109**

14. A girl who **goes** dancing every night must be popular. **96**

15. I am considered **to be** a model of virtue. **52**

Übung 71

1. If you change the job be careful. You may find that although the pay is better, the work is not so pleasant.

2. They are anxious to visit us because they think they're ill, and are afraid they'll infect us if they get near us.

3. There is only one beginner under them. The rest are experienced horseback riders.

4. It took him long years to regain his health.

5. The mother robin carried many worms to her always hungry babies.

6. Two years passed since he left his wife.

7. He'll be coming to Hamburg in the next time.

8. The young man insisted to build up his business without the financial help of his rich father.

9. The ugly old witch liked to eat him because he had tried to steal her magic ring.

10. It is without use to come early tomorrow because the boss won't be here.

11. My husband will overtake the management of the company when his father dies.

12. We were robbed from a teenage girl.

13. The package he received from Hong Kong was a real eye-opener. It contained a live snake, 10 feet long!

14. Is this bakery the best in town? Yes, I think.

15. There is nothing interesting on a foreign country if you only stay at luxury hotels; they are the same all over the world.

Lösung 71

1. If you change **jobs** be careful. You may find that although the pay is better, the work is not so pleasant. **106**

2. They are anxious **about visiting** us because they think they're ill, and are afraid they'll infect us if they get near us. **49**

3. There is only one beginner **among** them. The rest are experienced horseback riders. **116**

4. It took him **many** years to regain his health. **114**

5. The mother robin carried many worms to her **ever** hungry babies. **26**

6. Two years **have passed** since he left his wife. **108**

7. He'll be coming to Hamburg in the **near future.** **87**

8. The young man insisted **on building** up his business without the financial help of his rich father. **107**

9. The ugly old witch **wanted** to eat him because he had tried to steal her magic ring. **29**

10. It is **useless** to come early tomorrow because the boss won't be here. **115**

11. My husband will **take over** the management of the company when his father dies. **111**

12. We were robbed **by** a teenage girl. **86**

13. The package he received from Hong Kong was a real eye-opener. It contained a live snake, 10 feet long!

14. Is this bakery the best in town? Yes, I think **so.** **65**

15. There is nothing interesting **about** a foreign country if you only stay at luxury hotels; they are the same all over the world. **113**

Übung 72

1. I like being alone, and training my trumpet every day works wonders. No one ever bothers me while I'm playing!

2. She went to the party at first and asked for an invitation after she arrived. She had a reputation for being fresh.

3. Since the bills were sent out quite a long time ago and we have received no money already, we are going to sue for the money.

4. It is without use to speak reasonably to people who are always unreasonable.

5. Many people say if you are forty years old and yet in the same job, you will remain in it for the rest of your life.

6. The boy had not seen his mother in long years.

7. Because it was so late, the young man insisted to escort the young lady to her door.

8. It is nine years since I last saw her.

9. We are not all Germans for there is at least one American under us.

10. We'll prove if he's home before we go to visit him.

11. Since we came here, we had no sleep at night.

12. It was a mistake of us to let him join the club. The other members didn't want him admitted.

13. They gave us good advices.

14. We didn't know the man's name because we didn't meet him before.

15. What is interesting on this new educational plan is that it gives the students more freedom, but still helps them learn.

Lösung 72

1. I like being alone, and **practicing** my trumpet every day works wonders. No one ever bothers me while I'm playing! **39**

2. She went to the party **first** and asked for an invitation after she arrived. She had a reputation for being fresh. **112**

3. Since the bills were sent out quite a long time ago and we have received no money **yet,** we are going to sue for the money. **110**

4. It is **useless** to speak reasonably to people who are always unreasonable. **115**

5. Many people say that if you are forty years old and **still** in the same job, you will remain in it for the rest of your life. **109**

6. The boy had not seen his mother in **many** years. **114**

7. Because it was so late, the young man insisted **on escorting** the young lady to her door. **107**

8. It **has been** nine years since I last saw her. **46**

9. We are not all Germans for there is at least one American **among** us. **116**

10. We'll **check** if he's home before we go to visit him. **93**

11. Since we came here, we **have had** no sleep at night. **108**

12. It was a mistake of **ours** to let him join the club. The other members didn't want him admitted. **30**

13. They gave us good **advice.** **58**

14. We didn't know the man's name because we **hadn't met** him before. **31**

15. What is interesting **about** this new educational plan is that it gives the students more freedom, but still helps them learn. **113**

Übung 73

1. It is without use to tell him what to do. He won't listen.

2. There is only one lady under us; the rest of the people are men.

3. If you will consent to his wish, you will play right into his hands.

4. What for a notebook do you like best?

5. Ladies with curlers in their hair look like porcupines.

6. During the last years I've been sewing a great deal, and have come to enjoy it very much.

7. If you have no son to overtake your business when you retire, you must pick one of your employees to succeed you as manager.

8. While I asked him point-blank what he meant by his rude remark, he began to shuffle his feet and gnaw his nails nervously.

9. If you have not found the mistake in this sentence already, then your grammar needs some improving.

10. She thought he'd bring her flowers, but she was sadly mistaken.

11. He departed Hamburg with tears in his eyes for he knew he would not return for many years.

12. It takes long years to build up a business.

13. This house is made from glass.

14. He told her that he wanted to find everything ship-shape until the time he got home.

15. Although they had to steal very many cars at first, the bank-robbers found that it paid. By changing the car very often the police could not find out if they were escaping in a VW or a Mercedes.

Lösung 73

1. It is **useless** to tell him what to do. He won't listen. **115**

2. There is only one lady **among** us; the rest of the people are men. **116**

3. If you **consent** to his wish, you will play right into his hands. **37**

4. **What kind of a** notebook do you like best? **85**

5. Ladies with curlers in their hair look like porcupines.

6. During **the last few years** I've been sewing a great deal, and have come to enjoy it very much. **103**

7. If you have no son to **take over** your business when you retire, you must pick one of your employees to succeed you as manager. **111**

8. While I **was asking** him point-blank what he meant by his rude remark, he began to shuffle his feet and gnaw his nails nervously. **36**

9. If you have not found the mistake in this sentence **yet,** then your grammar needs some improving. **110**

10. She thought he'd bring her flowers, but she was sadly mistaken.

11. He departed **from** Hamburg with tears in his eyes for he knew he would not return for many years. **98**

12. It takes **many** years to build up a business. **114**

13. This house is made **of** glass. **90**

14. He told her that he wanted to find everything ship-shape **by** the time he got home. **69**

15. Although they had to steal very many cars at first, the bank-robbers found that it paid. By changing **cars** very often the police could not find out if they were escaping in a VW or a Mercedes. **106**

Übung 74

1. It's without use to try to make a normal child read before he's three years old.

2. The interesting thing on the marriage is that she is so beautiful and he is so ugly. The couple reminds me of Beauty and the Beast.

3. During watching television many people nibble on pretzels or cookies, yet they are often surprised about how overweight they are, and insist that they eat practically nothing at meals.

4. They've been ill more and more often during the last years.

5. The old man complained that he saw only his wife. He said he wanted to see someone other for a change.

6. There is no longer a frontier in America.

7. They asked what for a pine tree they had planted.

8. My grandmother wants to go on a picnic, but the weather is not warm enough for her already.

9. He did it at first and then asked his father for permission.

10. There's not a single stupid person under you in this room.

11. She told the police that she had seen him a year ago.

12. I won't criticize you if you have right.

13. He asked me if I wanted to take riding lessons, and I told him I was interesting.

14. When you don't come to work tomorrow, I'll call you at home.

15. After winning the case, she was so lucky that her lawyer had supported her through thick and thin, that she offered to marry him on the spot.

Lösung 74

1. It's **useless** to try to make a normal child read before he's three years old. **115**

2. The interesting thing **about** the marriage is that she is so beautiful and he is so ugly. The couple reminds me of Beauty and the Beast. **113**

3. **While** watching television many people nibble on pretzels or cookies, yet they are often surprised about how overweight they are, and insist that they eat practically nothing at meals. **105**

4. They've been ill more and more often during **the last few years.** **103**

5. The old man complained that he saw only his wife. He said he wanted to see someone **else** for a change. **94**

6. There is no longer a frontier in America.

7. They asked **what kind of a** pine tree they had planted. **85**

8. My grandmother wants to go on a picnic, but the weather is not warm enough for her **yet.** **110**

9. He did it **first** and then asked his father for permission. **112**

10. There's not a single stupid person **among** you in this room. **116**

11. She told the police that she had seen him a year **before.** **60**

12. I won't criticize you if you **are** right. **59**

13. He asked me if I wanted to take riding lessons, and I told him I was **interested.** **45**

14. **If** you don't come to work tomorrow, I'll call you at home. **53**

15. After winning the case, she was so **happy** that her lawyer had supported her through thick and thin, that she offered to marry him on the spot. **55**

Übung 75

1. He could never have got that position by his own effort because he's not very quick on the uptake.

2. We want that he puts all his cards on the table.

3. The guard locked the prisoner in his cell and left him alone in the dark.

4. Long years passed before the man was able to overcome the death of his wife.

5. It's without use to ask us for money because we have none.

6. Her hair-do is the same like my mother's.

7. Please overtake this job for me.

8. The two families haven't seen another for 40 years because they live so far apart.

9. At first he knocked at the door, then he looked in the window, and finally he sat down in despair on the porch step and waited.

10. It's quicker to fly as to drive, but it's more expensive. Which is the lesser of the two evils: much time or much money?

11. There are three presidents and one prime minister under them at the meeting.

12. The young man cannot vote because he is not 18 years old already.

13. The interesting thing on the fight is whether the ex-champion will be able to regain the title.

14. The purse of the girl was stolen while she was walking down the street.

15. If you aren't possible to convince her, forget it.

Lösung 75

1. He could never have got that position by his own effort because he's not very quick on the uptake.

2. We want **him to put** all his cards on the table. **50**

3. The guard locked the prisoner in his cell and left him alone in the dark.

4. **Many** years passed before the man was able to overcome the death of his wife. **114**

5. It's **useless** to ask us for money because we have none. **115**

6. Her hair-do is **like** my mother's. **43**

7. Please **take** this job **over** for me. **111**

8. The two families haven't seen **each other** for 40 years because they live so far apart. **63**

9. **First** he knocked at the door, then he looked in the window, and finally he sat down in despair on the porch step and waited. **112**

10. It's quicker to fly **than** to drive, but it's more expensive. Which is the lesser of the two evils: much time or much money? **56**

11. There are three presidents and one prime minister **among** them at the meeting. **116**

12. The young man cannot vote because he is not 18 years old **yet.** **110**

13. The interesting thing **about** the fight is whether the ex-champion will be able to regain the title. **113**

14. The **girl's purse** was stolen while she was walking down the street. **61**

15. If you aren't **able** to convince her, forget it. **64**

Übung 76

1. There's no good reason for our arguing about this. We're only splitting hairs, anyway.

2. When a forest fire wipes out a forest it takes long years to undo the damage.

3. The table was much too small for so many people.

4. The young pianist was so charming and such a good musician that he completely stole the show.

5. The couple was genuinely attached with each other.

6. I didn't even bother to ask him because I knew it was without use.

7. The most interesting thing on the transaction is the profit we will make, the least interesting the technical problems which will have to be solved.

8. "There is a traitor under us!" he cried.

9. Glasses and a beard make him look like a professor.

10. Her doll's house was made of cigar boxes glued together.

11. What for a lamp do you want to hang over the table?

12. At first she cried, then she screamed with rage.

13. During searching for iron the geologists accidentally came upon a rich deposit of zinc.

14. They all worked on English grammar until their heads ached, but when they were finished, they felt they had learned something.

15. If you have worked through every sentence in this book and are yet unsure about whether this sentence contains a mistake or not, you are beyond help.

Lösung 76

1. There's no good reason for our arguing about this. We're only splitting hairs, anyway. **74**

2. When a forest fire wipes out a forest it takes **many** years to undo the damage. **114**

3. The table was much too small for so many people.

4. The young pianist was so charming and such a good musician that he completely stole the show.

5. The couple was genuinely attached **to** each other. **97**

6. I didn't even bother to ask him because I knew it was **useless. 115**

7. The most interesting thing **about** the transaction is the profit we will make, the least interesting the technical problems which will have to be solved. **113**

8. "There is a traitor **among** us!" he cried. **116**

9. Glasses and a beard make him look like a professor.

10. Her doll's house was made of cigar boxes glued together.

11. **What kind of a** lamp do you want to hang over the table? **85**

12. **First** she cried, then she screamed with rage. **112**

13. **While** searching for iron the geologists accidentally came upon a rich deposit of zinc. **105**

14. They all worked on English grammar until their heads ached, but when they were finished, they felt they had learned something.

15. If you have worked through every sentence in this book and are **still** unsure about whether this sentence contains a mistake or not, you are beyond help. **109**

Grammatikalische Erläuterungen

Vorbemerkung: Das Problem eines unterschiedlichen Sprachgebrauchs, insbesondere der Schreibweisen mancher Wörter, im Englischen und Amerikanischen wurde undogmatisch gehandhabt. Der englische Sprachgebrauch (Schreibweise) wurde verwendet, soweit er noch vorherrscht, der amerikanische Sprachgebrauch (Schreibweise), soweit er sich als der gebräuchlichere durchgesetzt hat

1 Bei besitzanzeigenden Gegenständen benutzt der Engländer nie einen Artikel, da sonst irgendeine Hand, Tasche usw. gemeint sein kann und nicht die eigene.

2 Abgesehen von folgenden Ausnahmen (wenn das Fragewort Subjekt des Satzes ist oder bei Anwendung von – to be, can, must, have und may –) muß man im Simple Present und Simple Past ein Hilfsverb verwenden, wenn man eine Frage stellt.

3 Since wird nur verwendet, wenn man von einem bestimmten Zeitpunkt ausgeht. Zum Beispiel: He has worked in the office since 9 p.m. I have lived in this country since 1959.

For dagegen wird nur verwendet, wenn es sich um einen Zeitablauf handelt. Zum Beispiel: He has worked in the office for four hours. I have lived in this country for 13 years.

4 Hier handelt es sich um einen Satz, der zwar richtig ist, aber von Deutschen fast immer für falsch gehalten wird. Solche Fälle werden von nun an als "Difficult correct sentence" bezeichnet.

Die Form to have to wird tatsächlich häufiger als der dem Deutschen geläufige Begriff must verwendet.

5 Im Englischen haben Straßennamen keinen Artikel.

6 Who heißt zwar: wer, wird aber nur bei einer Frage verwendet. Zum Beispiel: Who has made this mistake? In allen anderen Fällen müssen die Wörter whoever oder he who verwendet werden.

7 Ein typischer Fall von verdeutschtem Englisch. Die einzelnen Wörter haben zwar die richtige Bedeutung, wenn man sie Wort für Wort übersetzt, aber im Satzzusammenhang ergeben sie Unsinn.

8 To make hat im Englischen meist die Bedeutung von: herstellen. Deutsche sagen oft: Das mache ich für Sie. Engländer sagen dafür: Das tue ich für Sie.

9 Well hat auch die Bedeutung von gesund; gesund schmecken kann hier aber nicht gemeint sein. Zudem gilt die Regel, daß die Sinne-Verben – to taste, to smell, to look, to feel – good and bad als Adverbien verwenden, niemals well and badly. Ein weiteres Beispiel: My dog has a good nose, he smells well, das heißt, mein Hund kann gut riechen. Mit: My dog smells good, ist gemeint, daß der Hund einen guten Geruch hat.

10 Engländer machen einen feinen Unterschied zwischen to listen to = zuhören, anhören und to hear = hören. I hear the radio, heißt also: Ich höre irgendwo Radiolärm; I listen to the radio: Ich höre einer Radiosendung zu.

11 To look at heißt: hinsehen, ansehen, im Sinne von: betrachten. Auch to see heißt: ansehen, aber im Sinne von: sehen, wahrnehmen, aufnehmen und sogar bemerken.

Zwei Beispiele: I looked at the girl and saw that she was ill: Ich sah das Mädchen an und bemerkte, daß sie krank war. I look at (watch) television and see a play by Shakespeare: Ich sehe fern und sehe mir ein Spiel von Shakespeare an.

12 Gebrauch des Continuous Present und des Simple Present. Continuous Present drückt etwas aus, das in diesem Augenblick geschieht: Beispiel: I'm eating cookies now. Engländer lassen meistens das Wort now weg, da das Continuous Present bereits das «jetzt» einschließt. Das Simple Present drückt ein Geschehen aus, das regelmäßig vorkommt. Beispiel: I eat every day.

13 Bittet man einen Deutschen um eine Übersetzung des Satzes: Ich habe meine Aufgaben gestern geschrieben, bekommt man oft zu hören: I have written my exercise yesterday. Dieser Satz ist im Englischen unmöglich, weil man niemals I have written mit yesterday in Verbindung bringen darf. Denn yesterday drückt eine abgeschlossene Zeit in der Vergangenheit aus, während I have written eine unabgeschlossene Zeit in der Gegenwart oder eine unbenannte Zeit in der Vergangenheit ausdrückt. (Diese Zeitform nennt man Present Perfect.) Das heißt, auf die Frage: Have you been in England? antwortet man, wenn man keine bestimmte Zeit in der Vergangenheit meint: Yes, I have. Wenn man eine bestimmte Zeit in der Vergangenheit meint, muß man mit zwei Sätzen antworten: Yes, I have been in England. I was there last year.

Ein weiteres Beispiel: Have you seen the film "Gone With the Wind?" (Present Perfect). Yes, I have (Present perfect). I saw it last week (Simple Past).

14 Any verwendet man bei Fragen und negativen Aussagen. Some wird bei positiven Aussagen verwendet. Beispiele: Is there any salt on the table? Yes, there is some salt on the table. Aber: No, there is not any salt on the table.

Eine häufig vorkommende Ausnahme: If there is anything I can do for you, I will. Obwohl es sich weder um eine Frage noch um eine negative Antwort handelt, ist anything in diesem Falle richtig, weil es hier soviel bedeutet wie: alles nur Mögliche und Denkbare.

15 Das Wort meaning klingt zwar wie: Meinung, heißt aber: Bedeutung. Das richtige Wort für Meinung ist opinion.

16 Gebrauch von also und either. Also und too verwendet man bei positiven Aussagen. Zum Beispiel: I can speak French and you can speak French too. Either verwendet man bei negativen Aussagen. Zum Beispiel: I can't speak French and you can't speak French either.

17 Difficult correct sentence. Der Satz wird von Deutschen oft als verkehrt angesehen, weil sie nicht wissen, daß man nicht nur who, sondern auch that als Relativpronomen verwenden kann, wenn es um Personen geht.

18 Gebrauch von ago und for. For heißt für (die Dauer von). Zum Beispiel: I learned English for two years: Ich habe 2 Jahre lang Englisch gelernt. Ago heißt vor. Zum Beispiel: I learned English two years ago: Vor zwei Jahren lernte ich Englisch. Das besondere Problem für Deutsche ist der Gleichklang von for und vor.

19 Equal heißt gleich, doch meistens im Sinne von: mathematisch gleich; auf keinen Fall aber ist es verwendbar im Sinne von: sofort.

20 Adverbs of time – wie generally, always, never, frequently, sometimes, often, seldom, usually – stehen vor dem Verb, wenn es nur ein Verb gibt: I usually eat lunch at noon. Bei Sätzen mit Hilfsverb und Verb stehen sie dazwischen: I have often eaten at this restaurant; bei Sätzen mit to be hinter dem Seins-Verb: I am usually hungry at noon.

21 Gebrauch von much und many, little und few. Much – little, more than – less than, the most – the least werden nur bei meßbaren Quantitäten wie Wodka, Zucker, Sand, Wasser, Geld verwendet.

Many – few, more than – fewer than, the most – the fewest werden nur bei zählbaren Sachen wie Flaschen, Groschen verwendet.

Außerdem muß man sich merken, daß man bei time und money immer die Wörter much und little verwendet. Das ist verwirrend, weil man in der Umgangssprache sagt: Count your money. Man zählt jedoch nicht das Geld, sondern die einzelnen Pfennige, Groschen und Scheine. Man macht also einen Unterschied zwischen viel Geld und viele Groschen.

22 Den Fehler in dem Satz: It is time for I to go home now, erkennt selbst der Anfänger. Deutsche halten aber sehr häufig die Verbindung for you and I für richtig. Sie prägen sich die als Subjekt richtige Verwendung you and I so gut ein, daß sie sie auch im falschen grammatikalischen Zusammenhang verwenden.

23 Gebrauch von me und myself. Myself, yourself, himself wird benutzt, wenn man für sich selbst etwas tut. Zum Beispiel: When things look very bad I tell myself they will soon get better. Unternimmt ein anderer etwas für mich, wird me verwendet: When my friends notice that I am down they try to cheer me up.

24 Adjektive müssen im Singular stehen. Wird das Wort million als Hauptwort verwendet, kann es im Plural stehen. Zum Beispiel: Millions of dollars were spent on the war. Man kann also sagen: The Tower is fifty metres high. Aber wenn man sagt: It is a fifty meter high building, muß meter als Adjektiv im Singular stehen.

25 Das Relativpronomen heißt im Englischen which und nicht what.

26 Gebrauch von always und ever. Die richtige Anwendung des Wortes ever macht Deutschen Schwierigkeiten. Die meisten Lexika übersetzen es mit: immer. Das ist aber nur in 5 % aller Fälle richtig, sonst heißt ever jemals. Ever heißt nur dann immer, wenn es als ein Adverb auftritt, das etwas über ein Adjektiv aussagt. Zum Beispiel: He is my ever-loving husband. Rex was his ever-faithful dog. Always wird immer im Zusammenhang mit einem Verb verwendet. Einige Beispiele: I always go home after the lesson. I always have lunch at twelve o'clock. I always shave before I leave for work.

27 Das unregelmäßige Verb to shine heißt: glänzen; es wird shine, shone, shone konjugiert. (Siehe auch 34.)

28 Entgegen dem deutschen Sprachgebrauch heißt es im Englischen nicht: How do you call this, sondern: What do you call this?

29 Vorsicht bei der Verwendung von to like to und to want to. Sie haben eine völlig unterschiedliche Bedeutung. To like to heißt: gern haben; to want to heißt: gern wollen, wünschen; to want to bezieht sich auf etwas, das man noch vorhat, während to like to sich auf etwas Gegenwärtiges bezieht.

30 Mine, yours, his, hers, its, ours, yours, theirs drücken den Genetiv aus.

31 Gebrauch von Simple Past und Past Perfect. Simple Past wird immer dann verwendet, wenn eine Handlung in der Vergangenheit abgeschlossen wurde, unabhängig davon, ob sie vor einem Tag oder vor Millionen von Jahren beendet wurde.

Bringt ein Satz zwei unterschiedliche in der Vergangenheit liegende Zeiten zum Ausdruck, wird der weiter zurückliegende Zeitpunkt im Past Perfect ausgedrückt. Zum Beispiel: Before Henry Ford invented the automobile, no one had ever ridden in a horseless carriage.

32 Nur wenn jemand oder etwas zu einem selbst gebracht wird (im Sinne von herbringen), heißt es auf englisch to bring. Wenn dagegen jemand oder etwas zu einer anderen Person oder zu einem anderen Ort gebracht wird (im Sinne von wegbringen), heißt es auf englisch to take.

33 Wenn man auf deutsch ausdrücken will, daß jemand nicht rechtzeitig erschienen ist, sagt man: Er ist 10 Minuten zu spät gekommen. Das wird meistens so übersetzt: He came ten minutes too late. Dieser Satz hat jedoch eine völlig andere Bedeutung. Too late bedeutet: zu spät, um etwas machen zu können; zum Beispiel, um einen Zug zu erreichen. Will man lediglich ausdrücken, daß der Betreffende ein wenig zu spät gekommen ist, aber im Grunde nichts versäumt hat, dann darf man nur sagen: He came ten minutes late.

34 Das regelmäßige Verb to shine heißt: polieren; es wird shine, shined, shined konjugiert.

35 To overlook heißt: etwas übersehen, im Sinne von: vernachlässigen, nicht beachten. To oversee heißt: etwas überschauen, im Sinne von: beaufsichtigen, überwachen.

36 Gebrauch des Continuous Past und des Simple Past. Continuous Past muß verwendet werden, wenn es sich um eine Tätigkeit in

der Vergangenheit handelt, die gerade im Gange war, als sie durch eine andere unterbrochen wurde. Zum Beispiel: While I was bathing, the telephone rang. Verkehrt ist ein Satz wie: I was bathing yesterday. Hier handelt es sich um eine abgeschlossene Tätigkeit in der Vergangenheit, die eine Verwendung des Simple Past erfordert. Wird die Frage gestellt: What were you doing when I phoned you yesterday, ist die Antwort: I was bathing vollkommen richtig, denn damit ist gemeint: I was bathing when you phoned me yesterday.

37 Gebrauch des Conditional (Bedingungsform). Der Deutsche drückt sich typischerweise so aus: The usher has told me, that if I will come to the theatre early, I will get a better seat. The usher told me that if I would come to the theatre early, I would get a better seat. The usher told me that if I would have come to the theatre early, I would have got a better seat.

Alle drei Sätze sind verkehrt. In einem Bedingungssatz kann nur einmal will oder would vorkommen, aber nie in Verbindung mit if. Richtig ist: The usher has told me that if I come to the theatre early, I will get a better seat. The usher told me that if I came to the theatre early, I would get a better seat. The usher told me that if I had come to the theatre early, I would have got a better seat.

Auf eine Benennung wurde hier absichtlich verzichtet, da die Vielzahl der Bezeichnungen für die Bedingungsform nur verwirrt. Wichtig ist ihre praktische Anwendung.

Der beste Weg, die Bedingungsform zu lernen, ist der musikalische. Man muß so viele Sätze in vereinfachter Form wiederholen (If I come I will get. If I came I would get. If I had come I would have got), bis ein If I would come I would get dem Ohr weh tut.

38 Leider klingen solche Sätze für das deutsche Ohr verkehrt, sie sind aber richtig.

I'm used to doing nothing heißt: Ich bin daran gewöhnt, nichts zu tun. I used to do nothing bedeutet: Früher pflegte ich nichts zu tun. I'm used to live alone ist doppelt falsch, weil es eine Mischung von used to und used to doing ist.

39 You can train your dog, but not your English. You must practice your English.

40 To stand heißt: stehen, to stay: bleiben. Man steht für gewöhnlich nicht 14 Tage lang am Meer, sondern bleibt dort für 14 Tage.

41 Difficult correct sentence. Who ist ein Wort, das sich nur auf Personen bezieht. Whose dagegen bezieht sich sowohl auf Personen als auch auf Gegenstände.

42 To become heißt: werden, und nicht: bekommen. Das richtige Wort für bekommen ist to get.

43 Gebrauch von like und as. Like heißt: wie, im Sinne von: ähnlich. You look like your brother. Dasselbe wie heißt dagegen: the same as; zum Beispiel: The color of your hair is the same as the color of your sister's hair.

44 Difficult correct sentence. Beginnt ein Satz mit einem negativen Präpositionsgefüge oder mit einem Zeitadverb statt mit einem Subjekt, müssen die Hilfsverben do, does, did im Simple Present oder im Simple Past vor das Subjekt gestellt werden. So heißt es: I seldom buy oranges in winter. Aber: Seldom do I buy oranges in winter.

Steht der Satz in einer anderen Zeitform, muß das vorhandene Hilfsverb vor das Subjekt gesetzt werden. Zum Beispiel: He will accept this offer at no time and under no circumstances. Aber: At no time and under no circumstances will he accept this offer.

Die Umkehrung der normalen englischen Satzlehre (Subjekt – Verb – Prädikat) verhindert stilistische Monotonie. Außerdem wird durch diesen Satzbau ein Teil des Satzes besonders betont, beziehungsweise besonders hervorgehoben.

45 Das Wort interesting heißt: interessant, gemeint ist aber: interessiert, und das heißt auf englisch interested.

46 Die Deutschen verwenden oft zwei Zeiten in einem Satz: die Vergangenheit und die Gegenwart. Im Englischen gibt es eine Zeit, die diese beiden Zeiten ausdrückt, und zwar das Present Perfect. Es wird verwendet, wenn etwas in der Vergangenheit begonnen hat, aber noch in die Gegenwart hineinreicht.

Im Gegensatz zum Simple Past (abgeschlossene Handlung in der Vergangenheit) drückt das Present Perfect eine Handlung aus, die in der Vergangenheit begann und in der Gegenwart fortdauert. Dies gilt zum Beispiel für Sätze mit this year, this month, this week, da alle diese Zeitspannen noch nicht abgelaufen sind.

Eine ausführliche Erklärung zu den wenigen Fällen, in denen man doch das Present Perfect benutzt, um eine in der Vergangenheit abgeschlossene Handlung auszudrücken, enthält die grammatikalische Erläuterung 13.

47 Difficult correct sentence. Der Imperfect von lie ist lay und nicht laid.

48 Verdeutschtes Englisch. Es heißt entweder near oder nearby.

49 Anxious heißt nur dann ängstlich, wenn es im Zusammenhang mit about steht und in Verbindung mit einem Verb, welches auf -ing endet. To be anxious to do something heißt nie: ängstlich sein, sondern: bestrebt sein.

50 I want that he ... ist im Englischen eine ungebräuchliche Ausdrucksweise. Richtig ist: I want him to ...

51 Still heißt zwar: noch, aber nur im zeitlichen Sinn. Das englische Wort für: noch, im Sinne von: sogar, heißt even.

52 Im Deutschen heißt es: Man betrachtet ihn als Verrückten. Im Englischen dagegen: I consider him to be crazy. Es ist möglich, das Hilfsverb to be fortzulassen.

53 Sehr oft wird when mit if verwechselt. When meint immer eine Zeit, if eine Bedingung. Das Problem für Deutsche ist, daß beides übersetzt wird mit: wenn. If kann zwar auch noch übersetzt werden mit: falls, diese Übersetzung ist jedoch weniger gebräuchlich.

Beispiele für die korrekte Anwendung sind: If I have time, I will see you tomorrow. Hier hängt das Zusammentreffen zweier Personen von der Bedingung ab, ob der andere Zeit hat oder nicht. Dagegen: I will see you when I'm through with work. Hier geht es nicht darum, ob man sich trifft, sondern zu welchem Zeitpunkt.

54 Difficult correct sentence. Das Wort since heißt nicht nur: seit, sondern auch: da.

55 Gebrauch von lucky und happy. To be happy heißt: glücklich sein, to be lucky: Glück haben.

56 As und than werden sehr häufig verwechselt. Beide werden übersetzt mit: als. Zum Beispiel: As I entered the room I saw a cat, oder: It looks as if ... Wird «als» bei einem Vergleich verwendet, kommt im Englischen as nur in Frage, wenn das Verglichene gleichwertig ist: I have as much money as you. Handelt es sich dagegen um Unterschiedliches, muß man das Wort than verwenden: I have more money than you.

57 Difficult correct sentence. Im Englischen neigt man dazu, alle Verben in die gleiche Zeit zu setzen. Das ist guter Stil. Niemand, der die englische Sprache beherrscht, würde auch nur auf den Gedanken kommen, daß etwas in der Gegenwart nicht weiter besteht, nur weil es in der Vergangenheitsform ausgedrückt wird. Findet man jedoch einen Satz, in dem zwei unterschiedliche Zeiten vorkommen, schließt er meist einen Relativsatz ein, der nicht stark genug ist, um die Zeit des anderen Verbs zu bestimmen.

58 Work gehört zu den Worten, von denen nur bei einer Änderung der ursprünglichen Bedeutung ein Plural gebildet werden kann. Weitere Beispiele sind: hair, fish, furniture, information, knowledge, sheep, advice.

59 Die Wendung: man hat Recht, darf nicht wörtlich übersetzt werden; im Englischen heißt es: man ist (im) Recht.

Zum Beispiel: He was right when he decided to stay home on that very cold night.

60 Gebrauch von ago und before. Ago wird in der direkten Rede verwendet, before meistens bei Vergangenheitsformen und in Verbindung mit der indirekten Rede: Suddenly he was famous. Ten years before no one had known his name.

61 Diese Form des Genetivs im Englischen muß man sich merken. Beispiel: The ideas of the people = The people's ideas.

62 Difficult correct sentence. In time wird nur verwendet, wenn man damit ausdrücken will: rechtzeitig, um etwas zu erreichen. Zum Beispiel: He arrived in time to see his friend. Will man jedoch nur ausdrücken, daß jemand pünktlich erschienen ist, heißt es on time.

63 Einander heißt im Englischen nicht another, sondern each other, wenn es sich um zwei Personen handelt. One another gebraucht man, wenn es mehr als zwei Personen betrifft.

64 Gebrauch von possible und able. Possible heißt möglich, able fähig. Man kann sagen: It is not possible. Man kann aber nicht sagen: She ist not possible. Als persönliches Fürwort muß man able verwenden.

65 Ich denke, es ist so, heißt übersetzt: I think so, und nicht I think it oder I think.

Die Kurzform der Antwort auf die Frage: Do you want to eat a pizza? heißt nicht: Yes, I want it, sondern Yes, I want to.

66 That what gibt es im Englischen nicht.

67 Man kann sagen: he kissed her, he killed her, aber niemals: he said her. Richtig ist: he told her, möglich, aber viel zu umständlich ist: he said to her.

68 Hier ist auf die Bildung des Subjekts genau zu achten.

69 Es wird **mindestens** bis zum Frühling dauern, heißt: It will take until spring. Will man aber sagen: Das Haus wird **spätestens** im Frühling fertig sein, heißt es: The building will be finished by spring.

70 Man kann it takes, muß aber I need sagen. Zum Beispiel: It takes me 5 Min. to prepare a meal. Oder: I need 5 Min. to prepare a meal. Viele Deutsche verwechseln auch to use mit to take; to use bedeutet verwenden, gebrauchen.

71 Der Deutsche sagt: Wenn das alles ist, was Sie brauchen . . ., der Engländer: Wenn das alles ist, das Sie brauchen . . .

72 To enjoy bedeutet: genießen, und nicht, wie viele annehmen: erfreuen (to please oder to like).

73 Die Verben must und to have to haben die gleiche Bedeutung. Must kann man aber nur in der Gegenwart verwenden, während man to have to auch in die Vergangenheit setzen kann. (Zur Erinnerung: Im Englischen gilt es, anders als im Deutschen, als guter Stil, wenn alle Verben in die gleiche Zeit gesetzt werden.)

74 Difficult correct sentence. Bei einigen Worten muß man den objektiven Genetiv verwenden. Beispiel: I object to your smoking.

75 To stay heißt: bleiben, im Sinne von: Er bleibt immer in seinem Zimmer. Bleiben, im Sinne von: weiterhin bei einer Sache bleiben, muß man entweder mit to keep oder to continue übersetzen.

76 «Kontrollieren» sollte man nicht mit to control, sondern mit to check übersetzen. To control hat mehr den Sinn von: lenken, steuern, beherrschen.

77 «Abhängig sein von» heißt auf Englisch nicht to depend from, sondern to depend on.

78 To visit heißt: einen kurzen Besuch abstatten. To attend heißt: besuchen im Sinne von teilnehmen.

79 All day heißt: den ganzen Tag. Every day dagegen: jeden Tag.

80 Das Wort interested erfordert die Präposition in und ein Verb mit -ing am Ende.

81 Das Wort then ist überflüssig und verkehrt.

82 It gives ist verdeutschtes Englisch. Es muß heißen: there is oder there are.

83 "In" wäre für das englische Sprachempfinden überausgedrückt im Sinne von: innen drin, was entweder selbstverständlich ist oder einer zusätzlichen Erklärung bedarf.

84 Eine weitere falsche Verwendungsweise von another. Anders, im Sinne von: unterschiedlich, heißt different.

85 What for gibt es im Englischen nicht, es heißt what a oder what kind of. What a hat die Bedeutung von: wie. Zum Beispiel ist mit what a great distance dasselbe wie how great a distance gemeint. What kind of wird verwendet, wenn es um Art oder Typus einer Sache geht. Zum Beispiel: What kind of dog do you have?

86 Die Präposition «von» mit der Bedeutung: gemacht von, geschrieben von, heißt im Englischen by.

87 In the next time ist deutsch, auf englisch heißt es: in the near future.

88 Die Ausdrücke to look after und to look for haben unterschiedliche Bedeutungen. To look after the beautiful girl bedeutet: auf ein hübsches Mädchen aufpassen, keineswegs, wie Deutsche meist meinen: einem hübschen Mädchen nachschauen. Das hieße: to look at the beautiful girl. To look for a beautiful girl, heißt: nach einem schönen Mädchen Ausschau halten.

89 Lautmalende Beschreibungen werden im Englischen nicht mit to make, sondern mit to go verbunden.

90 Die Präposition from bedeutet «von» nur im Sinne von: aus einer Richtung.

91 Gebrauch von both und two. Two gibt nur die Anzahl wieder, both wird stets ohne Artikel gebraucht und betont, daß beide Personen oder Sachen gleichermaßen betroffen sind.

92 Im Englischen drückt man ein Interesse nicht reflexiv aus; man sagt nicht: ich interessiere mich, sondern: ich bin interessiert an.

93 To prove hat die Bedeutung von: beweisen. «Prüfen» heißt to check oder to test.

94 Gebrauch von other und else. Beide bedeuten: anders. Else ist jedoch ein Substantiv, other ein Adjektiv. So heißt es: He said one thing, but he meant something else. Aber: The one man was French, the other man was German.

95 Ich habe einen eigenen Wagen, ist eine typisch deutsche Ausdrucksweise; im Englischen heißt es: I have my own car oder I have a car of my own.

96 Für Fragen im Simple Present und Simple Past, die eine Bestätigung oder Verneinung verlangen, gibt es vier Antwortmöglichkeiten: ein kurzes Bejahen oder Verneinen und eine lange bejahende oder verneinende Antwort. Nur die lange bejahende Antwort braucht kein Hilfsverb.

Zum Beispiel: Do you go home after the English lesson? Yes, I do. Yes, I go home after the English lesson. Oder: No, I do not. No I do not go home after the English lesson. Handelt es sich jedoch weder um eine Frage noch um eine Antwort, sondern um eine Aussage, wird kein Hilfsverb verwendet.

97 Married with heißt nicht, daß man mit jemandem verheiratet ist (married to), sondern daß man zusammen mit ihm verheiratet wird.

98 Bahnhofsenglisch: Ankunft und Abfahrt von Zügen und anderen Verkehrsmitteln werden oft unter Auslassung der Präpositionen ausgerufen. Im korrekten Englisch ist das nicht akzeptabel.

99 To remember heißt: sich an etwas erinnern, to remind (someone of): von etwas erinnert werden oder jemanden erinnern an. Zum Beispiel: If I remind myself often, and knot my handkerchief, I will not be able to forget.

100 Verdeutschtes Englisch.

101 Gebrauch von beside und besides. Beside heißt: neben, besides: außer oder außerdem.

102 There where gibt es auf englisch nicht, es heißt nur where.

103 The last years ist nur in Verbindung mit dem Wort of möglich. Es gibt im Englischen nur die letzten Jahre «von» diesem oder jenem. Zum Beispiel: The last years of his life were happy. Oder: The last years of the war were terrible. Dagegen gibt es den Ausdruck the last few years, der ohne of auskommt. Er ist im Unterschied zu the last years of sehr unbestimmt und besagt lediglich, während der letzten Jahre: The artist has not painted many pictures during the last few years.

104 Im Englischen kann man sich nicht wie im Deutschen selbst entschuldigen, man kann nur von jemand anderem entschuldigt werden und muß daher sagen: I must apologize oder please excuse me. Zusätzlich kompliziert wird die Sache noch dadurch, daß es die Wendung I excuse myself gibt. Das bedeutet jedoch: Ich rechtfertige mich.

105 Gebrauch von while und during. While wird vor einem Verb verwendet, during vor einem Substantiv. Zum Beispiel: While going down the street, I met an old friend. During the day I sleep.

While ist außerdem eine Konjunktion zur Verbindung von Haupt- und Nebensatz.

106 To change the plane bedeutet nicht, das Flugzeug wechseln, sondern es verändern.

107 To insist benötigt die Präposition on und ein Verb mit -ing am Ende.

108 Since kann man nur in "the perfect time" verwenden.

109 Gebrauch von yet und still. Yet heißt zwar: noch, wird aber nur verwendet, wenn man etwas negativ ausdrücken will. Zum Beispiel: He is not here yet. Still dagegen wird nur verwendet, wenn man etwas positiv ausdrücken will: He is still here.

110 Gebrauch von already und yet. Already muß bei positiven Aussagen verwendet werden. Nur bei negativen Aussagen darf das Wort yet genommen werden.

111 Etwas übernehmen, eine Aufgabe zum Beispiel, heißt nicht: to overtake, sondern: to take over.

112 Gebrauch von at first und first. At first hat die Bedeutung von: zunächst, und bezieht sich auf einen Eindruck oder eine Tätigkeit, die korrigiert werden muß. Zum Beispiel: At first I thought the color was red, but when I looked more closely I saw that it was a very dark blue. First dagegen verwendet man bei einer einfachen Abfolge von Eindrücken oder Tätigkeiten.

113 Im Englischen sagt man nicht, daß etwas «an» einer Sache interessant ist, sondern daß etwas «über» eine Sache interessant ist.

114 Verdeutschtes Englisch .

115 Engländer sagen nicht: it is without use, sondern: it is of no use oder it is useless.

116 Under us bedeutet nicht: zwischen uns, sondern räumlich: unter uns, zum Beispiel ein Stockwerk tiefer.